RESEARCH METHODOLOGY IN HISTORY

About the Author

Having started his teaching career at Himachal Pradesh University Shimla, Tej Ram Sharma, presently teaches History at the University of Hyderabad. He has served the University of Hyderabad for over two decades where he has been a founder member of the Department, Head of the Department of History, Dean of the School of Social Sciences and the Member of the Executive Council. He has participated, organised, chaired and inaugurated many conferences and seminars of Inter-disciplinary nature. He is a member of many National and International professional bodies. He has won wide acclaim from scholars for his earlier works and the prestigious awards conferred on him from the International Academic Community bear the stamp of a wider recognition of his scholarship. Presently he is working as a Professor in the Department of History and Coordinator of SAP-3, DSA-Department of History, University of Hyderabad.

RESEARCH METHODOLOGY IN HISTORY

TEJ RAM SHARMA
Professor, Department of History
University of Hyderabad

CONCEPT PUBLISHING COMPANY, NEW DELHI-110059

ISBN 81-7022-827-1 (HB)
ISBN 81-7022-828-X (PB)

First Published 2001

Printed and Published by
Ashok Kumar Mittal
Concept Publishing Company
A/15-16, Commercial Block, Mohan Garden
New Delhi-110059 (India)
Phones: 5648039, 5649024

Fax: 091–(11)–5648053

E-mail: publishing@conceptpub.com

Dedicated to the Memory of

My Father

Late Shri Kalidass Sharma

FOREWORD

I have great pleasure in writing this foreword to *Research Methodology in History* by Professor Tej Ram Sharma. This work is based on the author's decades of experience as a teacher, as an active researcher and a successful Research Supervisor. Professor Sharma, who has served this University for over twenty years, brings to his book not only his insights but also his wide reputation. I am happy that the book will be released during the Silver Jubilee year of the University.

The work essentially aims at helping a new researcher through various stages of research, from choosing a topic to the submission of dissertation. The emphasis all along is on quality of research. With focus on methods in research in history, Professor Sharma discusses the sources and related issues such as causation in history and objectivity in history in separate chapters.

I wish Professor Sharma every success with the publication as well as with his sustained scholarly pursuits in the field of historical research.

P. Rama Rao
Vice-Chancellor,
University of Hyderabad
Hyderabad - 500 046

PREFACE

The present work, *Research Methodology in History,* is based on my teaching this Course to M. Phil. and Research scholars for over twenty-five years in the Universities. I had to leave the book after writing some chapters a few years ago to concentrate on my duties and responsibilities as Head of the Department of History and Dean, School of Social Sciences in the University of Hyderabad. Some Indian and Foreign friends commented that these administrative positions will end in wastage of time and energy. However, I absorbed these comments in a positive way and dedicated myself to serve the Academic Community with all my capacities to get the best results. During my tenure of three years as Dean, School of Social Sciences, the research developed in leaps and bounds. More than fifty scholars earned their Ph.D. degrees (I made it a point to attend every *viva-voce* examination under the open viva system introduced during my tenure in the School) and over hundred candidates earned their M.Phil. degrees. I had a rare opportunity to scan through the Examiners' Reports in all the Departments and took keen interest in noticing the plus and minus points in the Theses/Dissertations. The results of this exposure are incorporated in the present work for the benefit of the new aspirants. This work could be completed with strenuous work on my part for the past few months after completion of my tenure as the Dean of School.

Any suggestion from the world of scholars, catering to the improvement of the present work, will be taken with a mark of gratitude and if possible, will be taken care of in the new edition.

I am deeply grateful to our Hon'ble Vice-Chancellor Professor P. Rama Rao for kindly writing a Foreword to the present work. I must express a word of gratitude to my daughter, Miss Richa Sharma, who helped me in finalising the Manuscript by carrying out the corrections on the computer and also for preparation of the Bibliography. In the end, I shall be failing in my duties if I do not mention the role of my wife, Brij Kishori Sharma and my son, Ranjan Sharma for bearing with me, thereby providing me solitude for long hours, for completion of the present work which had been kept in abeyance for more than a couple of years.

T.R. Sharma
Professor, Department of History
University of Hyderabad

CONTENTS

1

A WORD ABOUT HISTORY

History: Time and Concept

We have divided history into periods or time. Time is indivisible. We may talk of the concept of "TRIKĀLA" in this context. The Sages (*Rishis*) are known as *Trikāla–Darshinaḥ* i.e., knowing present, past and future, but we cannot define past and future. We may say near past or remote past; near future or future but we cannot explain clearly – it is vague, what duration it indicates? We have attempted to give some chronological frame-work or talk in terms of stages of human development, that also differs from country to country– there is no universal acceptance of division of time. Time is indivisible. We do not know where it started and when it will end? For a man, his time from birth to death may be his present, we do not know anything about his past or future–but man tries to see even in his present life, the past years as past, the current year as present and coming years as future.

Time–*kāla* derived from the root *kal* to calculate, can also mean to destroy and is seen in this second meaning as an agency of destruction, resulting in a negative eschatology.[1] According to *Yāska* (700 B.C.-500 B.C), *kāla* (time) is derived from (the root) *kal;* meaning to go.[2]

We have cosmological time described in the form of a *kalpa,* the longest period of time, consisting of 4320 million years and the four yugas – *kṛta, tretā, dvāpara* and *kali.* The kalpa which constitutes fourteen *manvantaras* is also known as the *mahāyuga.*[3] According to the *Vishṇu Purāṇa,* the *kali* age began after the *Mahābhārata* War, the date is recorded as 3102-1 B.C. "This was the date which came to be adopted in inscriptions and histories as well as where precise dates were required".[4] The learned Union Human Resource Development and Science and Technology Minister, Dr. Murali Manohar Joshi in his address at Hyderabad on June 21, 1998 exhorted Indian historians to adopt this date from the beginning of the *kali yuga* to be the date for rewriting the Indian History. Dr. Joshi elaborated this concept in Time and Space quoting the Sankalpa (pledge) which an individual took in any religious sacrament.

> "I, in the second half of the śveta-Varaha-kalpa, in the Jambū-Dvīpa in Bharata Khaṇḍa, in part of the Aryāvarta, in the pious place, the kaliyuga, in the first feet of kali, in such and such year, in such and such month, in such and such fortnight, on such and such date, such and such day of the week, born in such and such gotra, (mention the name of year, month, day, etc.) so and so by name (mention name), pledge thus".[5]

It has been alleged that the Indians believed in cyclic time due to follow up of the *manvantaras,* which repeated once again after the extinction, since time is eternal, *mahākala* which never ends. It may be observed that from the beginning of the *kaliyuga,* the concept of linear time also exists. We can locate the existence of linear time in Indian texts, such as genealogies, biographies and chronicles, where time-reckoning was recorded through generations, regional years and eras. It is suggested that cyclic and linear time were both used, but that their functions differed. Cyclic time occurs frequently in cosmological contexts and linear time in historical sources.[6]

It is significant that Pāṇini 500 B.C. made a distinction between the ordinary past and the distant past.[7]

Even Yāska quoting from the *Ṛgveda* 1/170/1 states about "today, tomorrow, the time that is still expected; yesterday, the time that has expired and is skeptical about the future who knows that which is not past? i.e., who knows that which is yet to come? (i.e. the future)".[8]

Actually time is indivisible, only we have divided it for our convenience. We may quote the idea of the unity of time in the 'past, present and future' by ticking of the watch every second from a Hindi film *"Kal Aaj Aur Kal"*(the three generations:- Prithviraj Kapoor:grandfather, Raj Kapoor: father, Randhir Kapoor: son) as follows:

> "Kal Aaj Aur Kal,
> Tick, Tick, Tick,
> Kal Aaj Aur Kal,
> Pal pal ki judati jāye kari"

Another idea which comes alive from the film is that 'the old order changeth yielding place to the new'. And after some time that new also becomes old and yields place to a new order and the process continues. That is what we see in history, study it and write about it.

Space, you can divide and define in particular, but not time in the rigid sense of the term.

History is not a bad word if we rightly understand it. It means an enquiry into what man thought, aspired, acted and achieved in the past; in short it is a record of total human endeavour in the past. An inquisitive mind is not simply satisfied in knowing what happened but also why it so happened?

When it happened, where it happened and how it so happened– which includes why it did not happen otherwise which could have happened other way as well. Thus this inquiry includes five "W"s– what, why, when, where and why not otherwise i.e., how it so happened? History is in continuity. It is a living subject – it never dies. The inquiry never ceases. The quest is eternal. It has no finality. It awaits new sources of information, new evidences and new conclusions. It is an interaction between the historian and his facts; not only that it is an interaction between historian and his readers especially the members of his own fraternity. It has no periodization which is only meant for specialization on account of human limitations e.g., Ancient History, Medieval History, Modern History, Constitutional History, Diplomatic History, Political History, Social History, Economic History, Maritime History,

Women History, History of Science and Technology, History of Movements, History of Art, History of Architecture, History of Painting, Tribal History, etc. which may be divided into various countries such as India, Pakistan, Bangladesh, Nepal, U.S.A., France, Germany, Great Britain, Africa, Thailand, Indonesia, China and Japan or taking the two together as Far East, as the case may be. It may again be subdivided into local history of a village, taluka, suburb, town, district, city, province, zone or region (such as North-Western India, Western India, Deccan), Metropolis and a country. To study the history of a vast country like India, one may again concentrate on Northern India or Southern India due to linguistic considerations. Actually the concept of history is universalistic or the world view of history – the local history conforms to town, town to city, city to province, province to the region and country at large, the country to the Eastern World – Middle East, South East Asia, Far East, Europe, Africa, i.e., from its original linkage or sub-division to the world at large. It creates interest in what was done in one part of the country or world or simultaneously done in different parts of the world, or how certain ideas of philosophy, science and technology originated in certain parts of the world and percolated to other parts and spread throughout the world.

However, hard one may try, one cannot delink the past. It equally applies to a country, civilization, society or a human being. This understanding has brought together all other subjects such as social sciences, arts and sciences, closer to history. You must know the basics of all other subjects to become a good historian. We now want to study history in the form of environmental and geographical factors. This has widened the scope, framework and horizon of history. The modern man (which includes women also) wants to measure the parameters and paradigms of human progress in the form of history of ideas, ideologies such as capitalism, colonialism and imperialism, the impact of science and technology on the evolution of human society in its various stages, the progress, the lifestyles and motivations of the advanced countries, developing countries and the Third World. Man has created various apparatus to satisfy his designs and achieve the objectives. History is the study in modern terms of the manoeuvring man, manipulative man who himself addressed as the super-man, which makes it all the more interesting, complex and varied. History is akin to literature in its presentation. It is not a dry and drab inventory of facts. The facts emerge out of analysis for which a lot of speculation, imagination and comparison is essential. You must speculate with various hypotheses, you must imagine the situation and compare your findings with the data. History merits its distinction as a subject of study; while other subjects throw light on the individual and specific studies based on their data, history talks not only of individual and specific but also general and universal, the world at large. It draws its experience and expertise from the times immemorial and specially from all the countries and parts of the world. Thus history is both a study of the unique and general.

There are unique persons, unique events and even unique countries (Na Bhūto na bhavishyati i.e., they were never before and will never be there in future). Many persons in literature, mythology and history have become proto-types of human behaviour such as Kaṁsa for cruelty; Kṛishna for diplomacy and sensual pleasures; Vichitra Vīrya alias Bhīshma Pitāmaha for firm resolve; Duryodhana for wickedness, Satyavādi Hariśchandra and Yudhiṣṭhira for truthfulness, Sītā and Sāvitrī for fidelity, Hanumān for service, Shravaṇa Kumāra and Lord Rāma for service to the parents, Nadir Shah for cruelty, Hitler and Mussolini for dictatorship, Saddam Hussain for stubbornness, etc.

Certain events in history are so memorable and incomparable to others such as the war between Rāma and Rāvaṇa holds no comparison with any other warfare (Rāma – Ravaṇayoḥ Yudham Rāma – Rāvaṇayohriva). Every event in history is a unique event by itself, whether it is First War of Indian Independence or the First World War and the Second World War. To clarify, we often categorize events into various forms such as mutiny, rebellion, crisis, movement, struggle, and War.

The United States of America is an unique country with unique people. It has been a melting pot where the most adventurous peoples from different parts of the world, who originally came here for the pursuit of money, gold and career got settled here as subject citizens. India is another unique country in so many respects. It is a pluralistic society comprising of people from many races, religions, creeds and many political parties. The separatist and fissiparous tendencies take their rise and subside. Again it resuscitates within from its own struggle and strength. On the basis of the study of literature, it has been pointed out that an American Literateur can write a novel or story which may have no connections with the past but an Afro-Asian man cannot get rid of his past and social moorings while writing in his genre. We, even in our nuclear families are part of the joint families; even living in modern age, we are rigidly traditional in so many ways as Indians. We need to study the factors which bind us to our home, town or province and restrain our thinking from becoming generous and liberal. We may speak in liberal and generous terms but we may act in the reverse. We converge around our narrow geographical boundaries and statehoods. This has to be changed to make our nation unified and great.

The Concept and Approaches to History

The concept of history has been changing from time to time. So also has been the record of human events varied in their choice, format, analysis and understanding[9]. The systematic and analytical approach to the writing of history is modern ; earlier i.e. in medieval and ancient periods, history had been written in the narrative form thereby indicating no proof or supporting evidence for what is being stated. It had a divine purpose and lacked humanistic approach. The narrative revolved around the strifes, feuds, struggles and wars between the gods and demons, semi-gods, demi-gods, royal dynasties, elite groups based on lay beliefs, heresay, magic and superstition. The mythology and folklore, which they called as oral tradition was included in the genre which was termed as "Universal History". No attempt was made to understand and analyze the events in contemporary writing.

With the establishment of numerous Universities and the Departments of History, therein manned by professional historians, the historian having proximity to other social scientists, scientists, linguists, archaeologists and philosophers, the benefit of printing technology, reprography, archives, museums, photography, tape recorder, television, and videography is at greater advantage than his earlier counterpart. But all this availability of resources makes his task all the more complex and difficult. He has to care for what others have stated on the subject.

The modern historian has ventured to analyze the events first searching out their sources and resources for information and then explaining them from the point of view of individual, group, society, the world at large and finally interpreting them with regard to different theories of socio-economic evolution, state formation and ideologies. For this he has started taking help from other disciplines such as anthropology, linguistics, archaeology, sociology, psychology, economics and political science. This has widened the horizon of history, enlarged its scope and confirmed its utility. The historians are studying history in all its aspects which includes different perspectives such as geographical (which is natural), environmental (which is man-made), cultural and social. In a democratic set-up the people at large cannot be ignored and have become equally or somewhat more important subjects of study along with the middle classes, elite groups and royal dynasties (which now-a-days have been relegated to the background). All this new scenario has created many diverse approaches (which are sometimes converse also) to the study of history. History is a record of all achievements and failures of mankind are a straight line definition of history. To understand the concept of history, we have to go deeper into the matter. We have to count and recount the aspirations and achievements and/or failures of an individual, group, nation and the world at large. We have to study how they act, react and counter-act with each other. Finally, more achievements take to domination of the superior and subordination of the other which may be taken at the individual, group, national and international level. To conclude, we may state that history is the struggle of human will to dominate or avoid domination, though subordination is the net result which is marked by silence, cooperation and obedience. The efforts to break the precipice are mashed by protests and reactions—both civilized and violent one followed by the other or both together. The urban folk culture has taken the Gandhian Philosophy of non-action and non-violence as constrained compulsion (*Majboorī dā nāma Mahatma Gandhi* in Punjabi). To quote a most recent example, the countries at large with a few exceptions, make proclaimed co-operation with the United States of America after having denounced alleged American efforts for their de-stabilization. With the involvement of the United Soviet Socialist Republics (Russia) in internal strife for democracy and economic crisis resulting in its weaknesses, the United States of America has emerged singularly as an unbridled Super-Power. The Russians are now, on the one hand, shaking hands with China while on the other hand are thinking to remove the word "Socialist" from the name of the country, though stating that would not mean leaving out the socialist path. This game of domination or avoidance of it works both at the individual, group, national and international level–which means the play or display of different forces at different levels. It depends upon our microscopic or macroscopic vision what we want to look at or study. It depends upon our individual, social, national and international interests changing the focus from time to time or as the case may be. This inter-play or over-play of forces makes the writing and understanding of history more interesting and difficult. This diversity has originated the diverse approaches to history which may be called the National, Utilitarian, Imperial, Marxian, Subaltern, Masculine, Feminine and we may club masculine and feminine under one name and call it the genetic approach, geographical, anthropological and psychological approaches to history. The phenomena is sometimes so complex that it cannot be covered or explained by a single approach or method and hence history has become a multi-method or multi-discipline subject, all at the same time, we cannot explain the events simply as a result of one single factor. There are historical perspectives, there are present factors or we may call them motivating factors for the events and there are precipitating factors or immediate causes of any event. The events may stop once settled at the initial stage but may recur again, may delay the course of action or be controlled temporarily or for some time duration. The etiology of causation is not limited to human element, the chance or invisible hand, also plays its vital role quite often.

Recent Debates in History

We find it advisable to review briefly the contents of a few important representative works in the field, to understand the recent trends and debates in history.

1. Georg G. Iggers, *New Directions in European Historiography* (Revised Edition) first published 1975, revised edition, by Methuen & Co. Ltd. London, 1985.

The work aims at projecting the changing methodological procedures, foci of interest and explanatory conceptions with the comprehensive assessment of present day historical scholarship "There has been a renewed interest in historical narrative, a revival of which at times directly challenges the new forms of social history but as often (particularly in its attention to the history of common men and women) reflects the new interests of the last several decades.[10]

The work has been divided into four chapters as follows ;

(i) The crisis of the conventional conception of "Scientific" history.

(ii) The Annales Tradition – French Historians in Search of Science of History.

(iii) Beyond "Historicism" – Some Developments in West German Historiography since the Fischer controversy.

(iv) Marxian and modern social history and finally there is an Epilogue.

History has been written for very different purposes and in very different ways, so that the borderline between history and myth, history and poetry, history and ideology has been a fluid one. Moreover, the days when historians could confidently write that "History is a science–no less and no more" are long past. However, until recently it has only seldom approached the history of historical studies as on - going discipline within its social and institutional context.[11]

The writing of a history which seeks to group meaningful connections among events and structures required a broader theoretical framework which made interpretation possible. For history to make the transition from erudition to a discipline which considered itself a science (wissenschaft), it was necessary that the critical use of evidence find its place within broader models of historical inquiry which, provided the conceptual framework by means of which the questions to be posed could be approached. These models were deeply rooted in the interests, view points, and intellectual concerns of the scholarly communities which employed them. Thus on the basis of a consensus of what constitutes evidence, very different histories could be written, different not only in their interpretation of a common topic, but different in their fundamental assumptions, approaches and style which closes the doors for any developments in historical scholarship. Every history ; it is argued, is valid only for the creed, party, class, nation, or age from which it originates.

Despite these divergences, the scope of historical studies has widened which includes the non-European world, giving a serious attention to broader segments of the population and to areas of human behaviour previously neglected. A broader agreement has appeared, shared by one and all that a history centering on the conscious actions of men does not suffice, but that human behaviour must be understood within the framework within which they occur. These structures often are hidden to the men who make history. History had to be placed on a sound methodological basis.

The historians of the twentieth century have remained committed to the critical use of evidence of the nineteenth century "Scientific" school yet they have recognized that the documents do not tell their own story which the historians of the nineteenth century followed in letting the past speak for itself, were generally insufficiently aware of the pre-suppositions which enabled them to establish threads of historical development. The result has been a strengthened recognition of the role which theories, hypotheses, and conceptualizations occupy in historical analysis and narration. No unified social or historical science has provided a fund of theory for historical explanation or guidelines for selection and organization of historical data. "Despite the profound differences and commitments which have divided historians, the continuous questioning of positions from within and from outside the community of historical scholars, intensified by the social, political and intellectual pressures of the times, has contributed not only to a broadening of historical perspective but to increasing methodological and conceptual rigor which has marked the human sciences generally.[12]

2. Keith Jenkins, *Rethinking History,* Routledge, London, 1991

Keith Jenkins opines that there is no definitive history as "history is basically a contested discourse, an embattled terrain wherein people(s), classes and groups autobiographically construct interpretations of the past literally to please themselves".[13] Jenkins provides great importance to the role of ideology in history which was hitherto missing. "In the end history is theory and theory is ideological and ideology just is material interests. Ideology seeps into every nook and cranny of history including the everyday practice of making histories in those institutions predominantly set aside in our social formation for the purpose–especially Universities."[14]

Moreover, history is being written for different reasons, one such being the professional history written by salaried historians, mostly employed in higher education and especially Universities are fraught with ideological framework, since they are occupying very dominant positions. Thus professional histories serve as expressions of how dominant ideologies currently articulate history 'academically'. They may disagree with each other about their findings for which they take shelter under certain technical vocabularies, categories, concepts and methodologies which are constantly being reworked. They work out a new history with traces of the past already known and with 'newish' material i.e., documents, records, artefacts etc, where the epistemological, methodological and ideological factors come into play before transforming it into a finished product. All such professional historians are subjected to various kinds of pressures from family, friends, work-place and publishing houses which put certain limits to their write-up, literary style and re-writing. Thus history remains a shifting and problematic discourse.[15]

The aim of historical study is to gain real (true) knowledge which is strictly speaking , unachievable. Each society has its 'general politics' of truth. "Truth is linked with systems of power which produce and sustain it."[16] If you understand that history is what historians make; that there are at least half a dozen sides to every argument so that history is relative. If it is all relative then Jenkins calls it 'hapless relativism'.[17]

It has been stated that historian's task is to discover not only what happened but how and why and what these things meant and mean which leads to construction of explanations. As historians transform the events of the past into patterns of meaning, it puts them into their limits.

As there are methods of finding out 'what happened' there is no method whatsoever to know what 'facts' mean. There are no central positions, but local patterns of dominance and marginality, which are all historiographically constructed and which must be historiographically read.[18]

The concept of historians' bias is everywhere, in schools, in history syllabi, in universities and even in any assessment of historical text. The bias is there in the reading of documents, primary and secondary traces and evidence. Someone may claim–that one can detect bias and expunge it by attending scrupulously to 'what the sources say'. But even if many historians use the same sources, still they come out with different accounts. When we study the history, we are not studying the past but what historians have constructed about the past.[19]

Similarly on sources and evidence, Keith Jenkins gives primacy to primary sources which he prefers to rename as original because originals seem genuine (true/deep) as opposed to secondary/second-hand traces. He calls the sources as traces of the past. Evidence is the term used when (some or other) of these traces are used 'in evidence' on behalf of (some or other) argument (interpretation) and not before. Evidence as opposed to traces is the product of the historians discourse on the past.

Similarly it may seem easy to explain the causes and

consequences of an event but actually it is not so to argue on cause and effect, continuity and change, and similarity and difference. Although these expressions are used by the historians all the time, Jenkins doubts whether they succeed in using them very rigorously. He gives the example of the French Revolution of 1789. When you combine the causal factors in terms of the various weight they may have exerted on some event, the question of their relative influence cannot be satisfactorily resolved.[20]

Historians learn to play the same game which others have played earlier and hardly deviate from the dominant discourse and are being inducted into a specific type of academic discourse. Hence Jenkins is skeptical whether these debates over conceptual couplets will be settled through the rigors of scientific method or the flair of the artist! There is no such thing as a single correct view as the historians with different orientations exhibit their differences on the *facts themselves.*[21] Moreover, the history itself has been written under diverse forces and pressures that can be understood by the practices and ideas of post-modernism. On which he devotes the final and third chapter of the book.

Jenkins states that post-modernism is a difficult area, as the post-modernists see nothing as fixed or solid. Anything can be made to look good or bad, desirable or undesirable, useful or useless, simply by being re-described. And it is this 're-descriptive turn' that we are interested in this text, the past/history. So the conditions of post-modernism have produced that multiplicity of histories that can be met everywhere throughout our democratic/consuming culture, a mass of genres (designer/niche histories) to be variously used and /or abused say historians' histories (professional histories attempting to exercise hegemony over the field, a version expressed in the thesis, the monograph and the text), teachers' histories (necessarily popularization of professional histories) and then a whole range of other distinctive forms that can only be listed; children's histories, popular-memory histories, prescribed histories, black histories, white histories, women's histories, feminist histories, men's histories, heritage histories, reactionary histories, revolutionary histories, bottom-dog histories, top-dog histories, etc, all these varying constructs being affected by local, regional, national and international perspectives. The past is played and replayed as an amusing range of styles, genres, signifying practices to be combined and re-combined at will. Thus a radical historicisation of history is necessary to arrive at an acknowledged position. Jenkins advocates for a series of histories to be written that helped us to understand the world that we live in and the forms of history that have both helped produce it and which it has produced; in other words not so much a history to help us understand the world in which we live then, but rather a series of 'histories of the present'.[22]

3. David Harvey, *The Condition of Post-modernity* Blackwell, USA, first published 1990. 1994 second edition.

The work is divided into the following four parts:

(i) The passage from modernity to post-modernity in contemporary culture.
(ii) The political-economic transformation of late twentieth-century Capitalism.
(iii) The experience of space and time
(iv) The condition of post-modernity.

There has been a sea-change in cultural as well as in political-economic practices since around, 1972. This sea-change is bound up with the emergence of new dominant ways in which we experience space and time. The culture of the advanced capitalist societies has undergone a profound shift in the *structure of feeling*. That there is a wholesale paradigm shift of the cultural, social and economic orders; any such claim clearly would be overblown. But in an important sector of our culture there is a noticeable shift in sensibility, practices and discourse formations which distinguishes a post-modern set of assumptions, experiences and propositions from that of a preceding period. We find writers like Foucault and Lyotard explicitly attacking any notion that there might be a meta-language, meta-narrative or meta-theory through which all things can be connected or represented. Universal and eternal truths, if they exist at all, cannot be specified. Condemning meta-narratives (broad interpretative schemes like those deployed by Marx or Freud) as 'totalizing', they insist upon the plurality of 'power-discourse' formations (Foucault), or of 'language games' (Lyotard). Lyotard in fact defines the post-modern simply as 'incredulity' towards meta-narratives'. According to Foucault, human body is the 'site' at which all forms of repression are ultimately registered and in Foucault's celebrated dictum there can be 'no relations of power without resistances'. He interprets Soviet repression as the inevitable outcome of a utopian revolutionary theory (Marxism) which appealed to the same techniques and knowledge systems as those embedded in the capitalist system it sought to replace. Foucault also rejects any holistic theory of capitalism. Harvey quotes Aronowitz arguing in *The Crisis of Historical Materialism* that 'the multiple, local, autonomous struggles for liberation occurring throughout the post-modern world make all incarnations of master discourses absolutely illegitimate'. The most appealing aspect of post-modern thought seems to be its concern with 'otherness'. Similarly, the author quotes from Huyssens (1984), who particularly castigates the imperialism of an enlightened modernity that presumes to speak for others (colonized people, blacks and minorities, religious groups, women, the working class) with a unified voice. *The idea that all groups have a right to speak for themselves, in their own voice, and have the voice accepted as authentic and legitimate is essential to the pluralistic stance of post-modernism.* Foucault's work, with marginal and interstitial groups has influenced a whole host of researchers, in field as diverse as criminology and anthropology, into new ways to reconstruct and represent the voices and experience of their subjects. A post-modernist will 'collage together incompatible source materials as an alternative to choosing between them'. The author quotes Pfeil (1988) who even goes so far as to depict the total field of post-modernism as ' a distilled representation of the whole antagonistic, voracious world of otherness'. He also cites Derrida who considers collage/montage as the primary form of post-modern discourse. The inherent heterogeneity of that (be it painting, writing, architecture) stimulates us, the receivers of the text or image, 'to produce a signification which could be neither univocal nor stable'. The author cites the example of Benjamin, a complex thinker in the Marxist tradition who worked the idea of collage/montage to perfection, in order to try and capture the many layered and fragmented relations between economy, politics and culture without ever abandoning the stand point of a totality of practices that constitute capitalism.

But if, as the postmodernists insist, we cannot aspire to any unified representation of the world, or picture it as a totality full of connections, and differentiations rather than as perpetually shifting fragments, then how can we possibly aspire to act coherently with respect to the world? The simple post-modernist answer is that since coherent representation and action are either repressive or illusionary (and therefore doomed to be self-dissolving and self-defeating), we should not even try to engage in some global project. Pragmatism then becomes the only possible philosophy of action.

The portrait of post-modernism seams to depend for its validity upon a particular way of experiencing, interpreting, and being in the world. This brings us to what is, perhaps the most problematic facet of post-modernism, its psychological presuppositions with respect to personality, motivation and behaviour. There is, in the post-modernism, little overt attempt to sustain continuity of values, beliefs or even disbeliefs.[23]

4. Norman K. Denzin, *Images of Postmodern Society,* Sage publications, London, First published 1991, 1993 edition.

The work is divided into two parts as follows:

Part one : *The Postmodern*
Part two : *Learning from Cinema*

Post modernism is defined by the following terms–a nostalgic, conservative longing for the past, coupled with an erasure of the boundaries between the past and the present; an intense pre-occupation with the real and its representations; a pornography of the visible; the commodification of sexuality and desire; a consumer culture which objectifies a set of masculine cultural ideals; intense emotional experiences shaped by anxiety, alienation, resentment, and a detachment from others.

The society only knows itself through the reflections that flow from the camera's eye. Members of the contemporary world know and see the themselves through cinema and television.

This suggests that classical, sociological ways of representing and writing about society require radical transformation. If sociology and other human disciplines are to remain in touch with the world of lived experience in the late twentieth century, then new ways of inscribing and reading the social must be found. The author states: "My topics are the self, lived experiences, and social theory in the postmodern moment. Three crucial identities, grounded in class, gender and race define the post-modern self. A single question guides my discussion: *How are these three identities enacted, and dramaturgically staged in the post-modern culture?* Phrased differently, "my project attempts to interpret how words, texts and then meanings play a pivotal part in 'those decisive performances of race, class and gender relations (that) shape the emergent political conditions (Referred) to as the postmodern world'. If the beginning of the post-modern period is marked by the end of the Second World War, it can be argued that each decade thereafter introduced and signalled significant changes which were then elaborated and articulated in the next decade. The postmodern World is characterized by the cultivation of conspicuous consumption consumer life-styles, already established under early capitalism, which stress the prestige and exchange value of appearance, civility, and personal pleasure and desire. The public self and its masks are increasingly defined by a media-oriented mass culture in which youth, health, and sexuality have taken on premium values. The popular culture of the past, especially film and pop music now define the present. The cool communication forms (satellite and cable TV, telex, fax machines), instant electronic communication (electronic mail) have produced a global village predicted, not on a shared humanness, but on marginality, and on cultural and racial differences. Controlled by multinational and state corporate structures, a satellite communications system connects the First and Third Worlds. This system articulates a set of popular culture ideologies which value family, sexuality, work and leisure.[24]

The New Historians

Journalists, politicians and advertisers are the new intellectuals; the new historians who have no sense of history, only meaning. The challenge to academics, artists and intellectuals is clear. These cultural intermediaries, who play to the market-oriented consumer culture, must be challenged and then messages deconstructed. These specialists in symbolic production constitute the new ruling class, or power elite. They have turned news into entertainment and then commentary into instant analysis. The dependence of these symbolic specialists on World economic system cannot be underestimated.[25]

In conclusion the author states that the major theories of post-modernism fail to live up to their promise. They still linger in the presence of the sociological classics, as they yearn to write a totalizing theory of this historical epoch. While concerned with the problems of representation and commodification of everyday life, they fail to develop a politics of resistance which would have global implications for the postmodern self who must confront the repressive features of postmodern culture.

Cinematic representations of postmodernism also fail to offer anything more then superficial solutions to the present conditions. When Hollywood deals with the class struggle, racism, or sexism, it perpetrates the myth that these obdurate realities can be overcome through luck or hard work. Contemporary cinema does not deal responsibly with these life situations.

The postmodern impulse is playful and paradoxical. It mocks and absorbs historical forms, always having it both ways, always modern and postmodern, nothing escapes its attention. Its logic of use and utility can turn anything from the past into a commodity that is sold, or used to sell a commodity in the present . . . .In short, capitalism needs and uses anything and everything to perpetuate its hegemonic control over popular culture.[26]

End of History and Clash of Civilizations

We may also take notice of the two often quoted works publicly by

Francis Fukuyama and the other by Professor Samuel P. Huntington of Harvard University reacting on the scenario of the post-cold war era. Francis Fukuyama in his 1989 Essay, The End of History? (which would grow into a book entitled: *The End of History and The Last Man*) argued that liberal democracy had conquered all the rival ideologies, the latest being communism which marked the "end point of mankind's Ideological evolution": The end of history.[27] In the 1993 summer issue of Foreign Affairs, Professor Samuel P. Huntington of Harvard University wrote an article The clash of civilisations? Which reminded that it was not the end of history, but that the major future conflicts will occur along the cultural fault lines between western and eastern civilizations. The Professor has removed the question mark but has made a massive and definitive elucidation of his argument in his latest work; *The Clash of Civilizations and the Remaking of World Order* (Simon & Schuster, 367 pp.) . Huntington states that the west is and will remain for years to come the most powerful civilization. As the west attempts to assert its values and to protect its interests, non-western societies confront a choice. A central axis of post-cold war world politics is thus the interaction of Western power and culture with the power and culture of non-western civilizations.[28] Nandini Sundar after taking a cue from Huntington's clash of civilizations has tried to apply this thesis in context of the Indian sub-continent where state interference in tribal customs with special reference to Bastar in Madhya Pradesh is generating trouble by disturbing their universe.[29]

As far as Francis Fukuyama's *The End of History* thesis is concerned we are informed that just after two years, he has sensed the shortfall in his thesis and has totally withdrawn himself in his work: *The Trust.*[30]

We are of the view that till society remains intact and the societies or human beings interact and react to each other, there will be no end of history whether we live in bi-polar world or uni-polar world; there are bound to be new permutations and combinations, new areas of conflict, new relations and new confrontations in the new world. Moreover, any wrong factual statement or discrepancy will be corrected by somebody or other.

So there will be no end of history. History will survive and continue till the world survives and continues.

Recent Trends in History – Writing in India

The colonial rulers tried to preach us that past is dead. But we are concerned not with pastness of the past but with 'pastness of the present' i.e. the living past. Our literacy tradition or history comes from our past or our culture not from outside as the British tried to impose their yearns or norms on us for our evaluation or presentation of the past. History writing is a living rather than a dead discipline– sensitive to new environment, new horizons, new complexities and newly developing perspectives. The 1990s have brought history writing to a new threshold: the Heritage History, history of ecology, of time and space, women, inter-personal relationships, perceptions, images and so forth. "This is happening in the community of historians around the world. It is, therefore, a sign of life among professional historians that they have been sensitive and responsive to the waves of change in the constitution of historical knowledge, looking at it increasingly as a very complex rather than a mono-causal process. Religion too finds a place in this complexity. Indian historiography has not only received these waves of knowledge but also contributed to them. The very fact of rewriting Indian History is a major contribution, for it alters perspectives on other parts of world history. But more specifically, subaltern historiography in India is the object of respect and source of inspiration for many such studies in several other parts of the world and one does not have to be a subalternist oneself to appreciate this".[31]

Archaeology and New Light on Ancient India

Professor Romila Thapar, presently chancellor of the University of Hyderabad had expressed her concern long ago that research work needs to be carried out to study the settlement patterns in a region which will apprise us of the changes taking place in Indian society from time to time rather then having picture of static socio-economic pattern in the following words: "It is surprising that, whilst work on Europe during the nineteenth century laid tremendous stress on discovering patterns of evolution in the history of Europe, the same approach was never applied to the study of Asian History. Indian history was treated as a series of islands in time, each named after a particular dynasty, and the same format was followed in most standard works by Indian historians."[32]

Happily enough Raba Ray made an attempt to study ancient settlement patterns in Eastern India[33]. Recently, one of my students Ms.M. Lavanya has attempted to study the pre-historic and early historic settlement patterns in Andhra Pradesh upto A.D. 500.[34] There is a dire need to take up such studies in other states.

Very recently it is being emphasized that an international approach should be taken up to study Indian history, treating South Asia as a whole (i.e. India, Pakistan, Bangladesh, Sri Lanka and Nepal) rather than restricting our scope to a single country or region. This trend is explicit in the following few works:

(i) Kishor K. Basa "Indian Writings on early History and Archaeology of South East Asia: A Historiographical Analysis" in *Journal of the Royal Asiatic Society,* London, Vol 8, 1998, pp. 395 – 410.

(ii) F.R. Allchin, *The Archaeology of Early Historic South Asia,* Cambridge University Press, 1995.

(iii) Jerome Jacobson (ed.) *Studies in the Archaeology of India and Pakistan,* New Delhi, 1986.

There are strenuous efforts being made by scholars and scientists together to trace the course of the Saraswati river which is no longer deemed to be a myth and which perhaps was a bigger river than the Indus and inhabited an earlier or contemporary civilization to the Indus Valley civilization. Recently a monograph has been published by Dr. S. Kalyanaraman on Saraswati Civilization:

Dr. S. Kalyanaraman, *Saraswathi (Sindhu) Civilization,* Saraswati Sindhu Research Centre, Chennai, 1997.

A team of scientists from Bhabha Atomic Research Centre (BARC), Trombay led by S.M. Rao have enthusiastically taken up the work to resolve the Saraswati mystery. Experts after, analysing the Vedic texts and remote-sensing images, agree that a river flowed through the Rajasthan desert. It was 1,500 km long and between 3 and 12 km wide.[35]

A historian has always to perform a formidable task of connecting the missing links and filling the gaps in the light of new findings, discoveries and researches.

Notes

1. Romila Thapar, *Time as a Metaphor of History : Early India,* OUP, Delhi, 1996 Second Impression, 1977, p. 6.
2. Lakshman Sarup, *The Nighaṇṭu and the Nirukta,* Motilal Banarasi Dass, Delhi, Reprinted 1984, p. 36.
3. Romila Thapar, *op. cit.*, p. 15.
4. *Ibid.* p. 29.
5. Vidyadhar Sharma, Madan Mohan, *et al, Nitya Karma Prayoga,* Gita Press, Gorakhpur, 1943, 19th Edition, (1988), p. 65; Hari Om tatsadyadyaitasya Śrībrahmane divitīyaparārdhe Śriśveta Varāhakalpe Jambūdvīpe Bharatakhande Āryavartaikadeshāntargate Puṇyakshetre Kaliyuge Kaliprathama Charane Amukamāse Amukapakshe Amukatithau Amukavāsare Amukagotropannaḥ Amukaśarmā Aham.........."
6. Romila Thapar, *op. cit.,* Passim.
7. Pāṇini, Āstadhyāyī 3/2/110 Lung Bhūtārthe dhātorlung : Bhūtāsāmānye i.e., ordinary past; *Ibid.,* 3/2/111, Anadyatane Lang: (i.e. distant past)
8. Lakshman Sarup, *The Nighantu and the Nirukta,* Motilal Banarasi Dass, Delhi, Reprinted 1984, p. 9.
9. T.R. Sharma, *The Concept of History,* pp. 9-23 and 75-113.
10. Georg.G. Iggers, *New Directions in European Historiography,* Preface to the Revised Edition.
11. *Ibid.,* pp. 4-5.
12. *Ibid.,* pp. 11-12.
13. Keith Jenkins, *Re-Thinking History,* Routledge, London, 1991. p. 19.
14. *Ibid.,* pp. 19-20.
15. *Ibid.,* pp. 20-24.
16. *Ibid.,* pp. 28-32.
17. *Ibid.,* p. 25.

18. *Ibid.*, pp. 32-36.
19. *Ibid.*, pp. 39-47.
20. *Ibid.*, pp. 47-51.
21. *Ibid.*, pp. 51-57.
22. *Ibid.*, pp. 59-70.
23. David Harvey, *The Condition of Post-Modernity,* pp. 40-65.
24. Norman K. Denzin, *Images of Post-modern Society.* pp. 1-9.
25. *Ibid.*, p.9.
26. *Ibid.*, pp. 150-151.
27. S. Prasannarajan, "Ancient Fears in New Age" *the Indian Express,* Hyderabad, Monday, May, 19, 1997, p.10.
28. *Ibid.*, cf., *The Indian Express,* Hyderabad Saturday, January 24, 1998 p.11; Spotlight All India Radio 18-1-98 9.15 p.m., Elusive International Relations". Based on Hungtington's thesis "clash of civilizations".
29. *The Indian Express Magazine,* January 24, 1999, p. 3.
30. S. Gurumurthy, Journalist and Financial Adviser to Indian Express in Seminar on *Economic Sanctions* at University of Hyderabad, Hyderabad Friday, 16th October, 1998.
31. Harbans Mukhia "Historical Wrongs" *The Indian Express* Friday, November 27, 1998., p.10.
32. Romila Thapar, *A History of India,* Vol I, Penguin Books, England, 1966, Reprinted 1982, p. 20.
33. Reba Roy, *Ancient Settlement Patterns in Eastern India,* Calcutta, 1987.
34. M. Lavanya, Pre-Historic and Early Historic Settlement patterns in Andhra Pradesh upto A.D. 500. An unpublished Ph.D. thesis University of Hyderabad, 1998.
35. "Saraswati's no Myth" *Indian Express,* Express Magazine May, 9, 1999 p.2, a review article by Pallava Bagla.

2

RESEARCH IN HISTORY

There should be thrill in research. The thrill comes with new insights provided by the guide, new discovery of facts and new interpretation if convincing.

Research : knowing categorically about something.

What is Research?

Research is an academic pursuit based on thorough knowledge of the subject or topic of research previously combined with new findings and new data if any. It should provide either new interpretation of the old data if it is already furrowed field or entirely based on the new data as the case my be if it is a fresh exploration on the epigraphy, numismatics, art and architecture or a new personality.

Attributes of a good research work

The following points need our attention for a research work of quality:

1. There should not be any inexcusable factual error.
2. There should be proper consideration of spatial and temporal dimensions.
3. There should be coherence of facts.
4. There should be linkage of subject matter and discussion.
5. The unit or area of analysis should be identified, defined and concentrated upon during the discussion.

6. The total piece of writing should not be a disjointed product.
7. The footnoting and reference works should be properly done as per norms of the discipline.

To achieve the above mentioned ends the following tips are given to the researcher

1. You must collect all the available data on the subject of your choice. No one should neglect, on any ground whatsoever, any particular class of data, or deliberately avoid reference to them, when they go against any preconceived theory or view.[1]
2. In collection, interpretation and concluding the evidence of facts you need to perform the duties of a judge rather than acting like an advocate.[2]
3. You must divest your mind of sentiments, prejudices and preconceptions and all kinds of human emotions, which are likely to distort your vision and judgement. The merit of a historian is to be judged in how far he conforms to this ideal.[3]
4. You must watch carefully your own methods as well as the vagaries of the material on which you are working.[4]
5. A historian must take a professional oath of "searching the truth and working for truth alone" like the Hippocratic Oath gone for by medical students and practitioners of "using the knowledge acquired for the service of humanity at large and not for the purposes of exploiting it at any cost". To quote the words of Niebuhr who said "In laying down the pen, we must be able to say in the sight of God: I have not knowingly nor without earnest investigation written anything which is not true"[5]. The same idea is more beautifully put in the words of Sir Jadunath Sarkar while addressing a historical conference in Bengal of which the following literal English translation of the original Bengali passage has been put forth by Majumdar. "I would not care whether truth is pleasant or unpleasant, and in consonance with or opposed to current views. I would not mind in the least whether truth is or is not a blow to the glory of my country. If

necessary, I shall bear in patience the ridicule and slander of friends and society for the sake of preaching truth. But still I shall seek truth, understand truth, and accept truth. This should be the firm resolve of a historian."[6]

It is equally important to illustrate the point further to spotlight the shortfalls/defects in the dissertations/theses as pointed out by the examiners usually in the evaluation reports of M.Phil dissertations/ Ph.D. Theses.

Short Falls/ Defects in the Dissertations/Theses

1. The aims and objectives of the research topic are not properly highlighted.
2. The methodology is vague and not properly defined. It should not exhibit empty or tall claims by the author.
3. There is no sufficient discussion on the previous literature on the topic or area of studies, methodology followed by various authors, merits and demerits of the previous works done in the field of study i.e., a critique on the historiography of the topic and the desideratum for the present work in clear and concrete terms.
4. There is no cohesiveness of one chapter with the succeeding chapter(s). Sometimes the examiners have pointed out a particular chapter being out of place or have recommended an abridgement of it, being very lengthy or out of proportion to fit in the context.
5. There is no rationale in the argument, not being substantiated by the data provided with or conclusions being drawn from analysis of the data are not in tune with it; hasty, wilful and arbitrary conclusions are being drawn without any sound basis which may be deemed as far-fetched by the reader. Quite often some sweeping statements mar the beauty of the thesis as such statements have been made without any foundation or supporting evidence or having a data-base.

6. The concepts followed or terminology used by the author is not properly known or clear to the author himself.
7. The books or works quoted in the body of the thesis are found missing in the Bibliography.

The Classification of Research

Research has often been classified into two forms as pure and applied. While the former contributes to the general pool of knowledge, the latter helps the solution of many a complex problems of society. There is no clear-cut demarcating line between the two as all research can be applied research in some sense of the term. The controversy over the fundamental versus applied research is largely academic.[7]

Research and Folklore

Research is a hard pursuit to follow, especially the historical research where you never feel to complete your data and often find yourself in wilderness, lost in the maze of facts as you have to elaborate your point not only from manifold sources but also to cite various authorities on the subject. It needs perseverance, patience, thoughtfulness, imagination and above all, the skill of the craft. It is not green pastures for everybody. It is not everybody's cup of tea. A haphazard approach, half-hearted efforts, hasty data and hasty conclusions will throw everything to the dustbin. I remember how my research guide during my research career advocated concerted efforts on my part in the following words. "You should not go for marriage. Research herself is a jolly mistress which needs your full attention".

During our times, in good old days, when we pursued research work leading to a Ph. D. degree, there were no courses offered on the Research Methodology as the present days by the Universities. Once I enquired my research guide "What is this *Ibid.*, which is quite often quoted in footnotes?". He told me a tit-bit that earlier some research scholar had asked the same question to his research guide in some university in a different way. "Who is this author

Ibid. Who seem to have authored many books and is quoted by everybody?". As we know that the same authority, the same book and the same page number is not mentioned again in the same words which is shown by the word *'Ibid'* as many times as it is necessary to do so if it is without any other intervening footnote.

Research degree is a prescribed necessary qualification for a teaching career in a Degree College or a University. It is taken as a ladder for success and promotion in the career. It is quite often followed by its own hazards and pitfalls which are many; to mention a few – lack of guidance, scarcity of source material, abundance of source material, late knowledge of somebody else working on the same topic or late realization of the futility of the topic itself, or lack of skill for tapping the sources, lack of cooperation from the research guide when the work is in progress, lack of funds, last but not the least to mention non-cooperation at times by the typist or his shortfalls which are equally crucial for a neat presentation. It was nevertheless very much less attractive in earlier days when there were only a few fellowships, that too of small value, while in modern times, it has been made little more attractive by opening up Fellowships by the Indian Council of Historical Research, Indian Council of Social Science Research and specially by organizing the JRF Examinations and Qualifying Test for University Lecturers at National level by the University Grants Commission, New Delhi. Still the settlement in career is delayed by five to seven years in comparison to other jobs if one can get through the competitive examination conducted by various recruiting agencies. Still some people pursue it and pursue it now with some degree of fondness. Hence the folklore : Once two donkeys met each other and shared each other's welfare and whereabouts. The first donkey was employed by a washerman for whom he took his bundle of clothes to the ghats in the morning where he enjoyed fresh air and drank plenty of water as he required. He had no other work once he brought the washed out and dried clothes back home. He took full rest gazing the starry nights and enjoyed full sleep till he got up next morning. The second donkey happened to work in a circus. He was given to carry enough work loads during the day and work for the nights in the circus. For all this hard work and labour he was provided with insufficient diet. The former suggested the latter one to shift to a washerman by leaving the circus owner. To which the latter retorted "But my future is bright. There is a sweet sixteen years young girl in the circus who has to do tight rope walking whom the owner tells "Caution, little girl, the day you slip down the rope, I shall marry you to this donkey". Thus the second donkey abjured the suggestion of the first donkey for immediate betterment of his life.

Uses of Research

Onc use of the research is leading to the award of Ph.D. (Doctor of Philosophy) degree thus qualifying for a job in a research organization or in a University. After the candidate has presented his research work, it is sent for evaluation to the examiners who in due course send their reports. In most of the universities, two outside experts are appointed as examiners. If the reports are unanimously positive, after the screening of the reports the candidate is exposed to a *Viva-Voce* examination where the Board recommends the award of the degree. In case one of the examiners dissents the award of the degree, a third examiner is appointed. In some Universities to avoid the hassles of a third examiner, three outside experts are appointed as examiners in the first instance. If the reports of the two of them atleast are favourable, after screening of the reports, the *Viva-Voce* examination is conducted for the candidate. After the satisfying performance, the candidate is recommended for the award of the degree by the university. The award of the degree should not be taken as the *summum bonum* of life which usually is the case with the candidates. Actually the award of the degree is a beginning, certifying the candidate's potential or capacity for research which he should follow up.

There are other research works of lesser degree leading to M.Phil (Master of Philosophy) degree so called M.Phil dissertations. Most of them cover a small area and are not of considerable wealth. A large number of them just gather dust in the shelves of the libraries. With the termination of the study, the topics are left out as they are without covering a larger dimension though some of them are not worth consideration for the purpose. The universities should circulate their annual list with the topic, method and approach as well as the gist of the subject matter and a bigger list should be published every decade. Little effort in this direction, to publish the list of the accepted doctoral theses by the universities is made by the Association of Indian Universities, New Delhi, in their magazine *University News* along with the topics registered for Ph.D. degree by various universities, though the latter part is perhaps not taken seriously by most of the universities as is apparent, if the response shown in their publication by the magazine is an index. The other effort made in this direction by publication of a Bulletin on Survey of Research in Social Sciences in South India by the Madras Institute of Developmental Studies, Madras, where also the lack of response on the part of many universities is apparent. A survey of research work in history completed /or in process can be taken upon at the national level by the Indian Council of Historical Research.

Worst is the case with the survey reports and research projects carried out by individuals which are gathering dust in department shelves only to be eaten up by insects finally.

Similarly, the research works in regional languages as has been permitted in some universities lacks circulation and utility. Some way has to be found out to properly utilize their talent at the national level. There is no use of research which does not add to the general pool of knowledge.

There is a wide gap for circulation of new findings. Any advancement in knowledge should percolate down to the schools. The NCERT (National Council of Educational Research and Training) has made some concerted efforts in this direction but still much more needs to be done.

We need to coordinate and collaborate at national level to concentrate all these scattered rays of light into one focus, to make a synthesis of all our special treatises and researches in Indian history. Sir Jadunath Sarkar has rightly quoted Professor Patrick Geddes while reminding us of this urgent need of the time. "We have plenty of spinners, who have produced fine threads. We now want a master weaver who will synthesize all these isolated facts. That the crying need of the modern World of Science: Weave! Weave!"[8]

Teaching and Research

Let us consider for a while why a research degree has been made a pre-requisite for a teaching job in an institution of higher education or a university? It is a training in philosophizing a topic, going into deeper details which involves a thinking process and rationalization of the issues concerned with the problems. This is necessary to give life to the subject you are teaching whether it is political history, socio-economic history, history of ideas, peasant studies, women studies, art and architecture, historiography or socio-religious and reform movements, freedom struggle, nationalism and imperialism, so on and so forth. You must conceptualize, rationalize and then teach it.

Some teachers over emphasize teaching work, especially those who never qualified themselves for a research degree or those who bade a goodbye to research work after they earned a research degree. In fact research and teaching go together. In the United States of America there are no promotional avenues for a teacher who forsakes research; the slogan is "Publish or Perish". In India this marked distinction is ignored. To provide due incentives to research work, it is necessary to create a special cadre of *Research Professors* who have distinguished themselves as researchers and research guides and to put them in a higher scale than other Professors. A national effort of planning and organization of the cadre at middle level is more essential than nominating or selecting a few scholars as National Professors.

Quality of Research

A few words about the quality of research carried out in our universities will not be out of place. 'We hear today a good deal about the absurdities of minute research, especially in Ph.D. thesis'. It is very difficult to say what is important and what is superfluous in such exercises. We are not expected to evaluate them by our own standards. G.R.Elton takes a liberal view of the laborious work done by a budding scholar. "Research work of this journeyman kind deserves to be judged by the only tests it seeks to satisfy: it is honest and exhaustive, has it asked questions that are right and adequate in the context of the problem, has it found reasonable answers, does it prove the author to have learned his trade? And much the same applies beyond the stage of the Ph.D. Dissertation, good and bad work can be done at all stages of enterprise, the standard of quality to apply must be defined as intellectual honesty and intellectual penetration within the compass of the problem investigated"?.[9] We may not agree with Elton when he criticizes Mr. Carr and others who think like him, but would judge by the purpose which a piece of historical writing is meant to serve.[10] A historical writing must serve some purpose. A brilliant student must venture on some more important topic which may have more social relevance for the present. It is no use taking up some topics which have become obsolete but may have some relevance to history in general. No topic may be totally useless but we must have a choice for the better one.

Role of Professional and Allied Organisations

Fortunately enough, the number of professional bodies in historical studies is quite large in comparison to any other subject of study whether in Arts, Social Sciences or even in Sciences. The other subjects may only envy it on this point. To mention a few of them, namely, Royal Asiatic Society of Great Britain and Ireland with branches at Calcutta and Bombay (Bombay Branch is being revived by the concerted efforts of Prof. Sardesai), International Congress of Human Sciences in Asia and North Africa (Former International Congress of Orientalists), Association of South Asian Archaeologists in Western Europe, Archaeological Survey of India, Indian Council of Historical Research, National Museum, New Delhi (has become a deemed University), Indian History Congress, Archaeological Society of India, All India Oriental Conference, Itihasa Samshodhana Mandala, Poona; Numismatic Society of India, Epigraphical Society of India, Place-Name Society of India, Indian Social Science Congress, South Indian History Conference,

Numismatic Society of South India (recently formed), Andhra Pradesh History Congress, Punjab History Conference, Rajasthan History Congress, Tamilnadu Council of Historical Research, Kerala Historical Society, Kerala Historical Association, Calcutta Historical Society, Madhya Pradesh Itihas Parishad, Assam Historical Society, Kalinga Historical Society, Orissa Historical Society, Bihar Itihas Parishad, Institute of Historical Studies, Calcutta, Institute of Archaeology, A.S.R., New Delhi, Bhandarkar Oriental Research Institute, Poona; Vishveshwaranand Institute of Indological Studies, Hoshiarpur, Kuppuswami Sastri Research Institute, Mylapore, Madras-600 004, Indian Institutc of Rcscarch in Numismatic Studies, Nasik, Mythic Society of India, Bangalore; Indian Institute of Advanced Study, Shimla; etc.

Except for the International Congress which is held every two years, most of the above mentioned societies conduct their annual conferences where research papers are read on relevant topics and the proceedings published every year. Some of them even issue their Research Journals, such as the *Journal of the Royal Asiatic Society* of Great Britain and Ireland, *The Indian Historical Review* (Indian Council of Historical Research, New Delhi), *Archaeology – A Review* (Archaeological Survey of India, New Delhi), *Journal of the Numismatic Society of India,* Banaras Hindu University, Varanasi, *Journal of the Mythic Society of India,* Bangalore, *The Quarterly Review of Historical Studies,* (Institute of Historical Studies, Calcutta), *Vishveshawaranand Indological Journal* (Vishveshwaranand Institute of Indological Studies, Hoshiarpur). Apart from that, we may also mentioned the *Journal of the Oriental Institute,* Baroda; *Deccan College Research Bulletin* (Deccan College, Poona) and *Puranam* (Published by Maharaja Kashiraj Trust, Ramnagar, Varanasi).

A few other important journals are *Indica,* Heras Institute, St. Xavier's College Bcmbay, *Ancient India, Annals of the Bhadarkar Oriental Research Institute, Social Scientist, Bulletin of the School of Oriental and African Studies,* London. *The Journal of Peasant Studies*, London, *Indian Antiquary, Indian Historical Quarterly, Islamic Culture,* Hyderabad, *Journal of the American Oriental Society, Journal of the Economic and Social History of the Orient.*

Netherlands, *Journal of Indian History,* Trivandrum, *Journal of the Bihar Research Society, Man in India,* Man, London, *Indian Culture : The Quarterly Review of Historical Studies,* Institute of Historical Studies, Calcutta, *Indo-British Review,* Madras, *A Journal of History, Current History, Comparative Studies in Society and History,* Cambridge University Press; *The Medieval History Journal, Indian Economic and Social History Review, Indian Journal of Social Science, South Asia Journal* and *Studies in History* (All published by Sage Publications India Pvt. Ltd., Post Box 4215, New Delhi 110 048) and *Ithihas* (Journal of the Andhra Pradesh State Archives, Hyderabad 500 007), *The Journal of Archaeology* published by the Government of Andhra Pradesh, Hyderabad). There may be other research journals published by various Universities such as *Punjab University Research Journal,* Chandigarh and *Banaras Hindu University Research Journal (Prajna), Journal of Contemporary History,* Sage Publications, *European History Quarterly,* Sage Publications, *Folklore,* Calcutta, *Antiquity,* Oxford University Press.

American Studies Research Centre, Hyderabad-500 007 which was inaugurated on April 4, 1964[11] is doing good services to American studies by publishing the *The MLA Style Sheet, Fundamentals of Research.* It also publishes the *Indian Journal of American Studies.* Not only that, it takes pains by publication of *Ideas* Indian Doctoral Engagements in American Studies every two years, which provides us with a two page brief of the topic along with scheme of chapterisation. Recently University of Hyderabad has brought out a Handbook containing Doctoral Theses 1982-1997. Andhra Pradesh History Congress 22nd session held under the auspices of the Department of History, School of Social Sciences, University of Hyderabad 10-11 January, 1998 *Souvenir* has published a list of research works done and ongoing in the Department of History, University of Hyderabad.

Role of Indian Council of Historical Research

Indian Council of Historical Research (ICHR) manned by eminent historians has taken upon itself to play a pivotal role in the organization of historical research. It has organized seminars and symposia on important themes from time to time. It organizes, sponsors and supports the seminars, workshops and conferences for the promotion and utilization of historical knowledge. It awards fellowships and sanctions grants for research projects as well as provides financial help for the publication of theses, manuscripts/ journals. It has evolved schemes to collect the source materials in the form of inscriptions, translations of important and rare books, preparations of catalogues, editing texts, political and social movements, collection of economic and statistical data and preparation of old Zamindari records. It has identified scholars and allotted them the responsibility for compilation and preparation of such source materials. Some work is completed while the rest is on the way to completion. It has published some works originally published in English into Hindi and other regional languages, some original works in English while some edited works by various scholars are under print. It prints a journal entitled *The Indian Historical Review,* which contains some leading articles, review articles and review of books. Actually more than half of the space in the journal is consumed by the Book Reviews. The experts in different fields are contacted without any bias to review the books in their area of specialization. It also issues a *Newsletter* which furnishes us with some information on the research projects undertaken, research grants, publications and other activities. But unfortunately this *Newsletter* is not given a wide circulation, it is only given or sent on demand.

In fact, the Indian Council for Historical Research should bring out a yearly publication containing information on Doctoral engagements in the universities on the lines of *Ideas,* Indian Doctoral Engagements in American Studies, published by American Studies Research Centre, Hyderabad as mentioned earlier.

Role of the University Grants Commission, New Delhi

The University Grants Commission (UGC) is the premier body which gives recognition to any institution as university or deemed University, delivers grants to the universities, sets up and maintain standards of all the branches of knowledge, admits certain Department in the Universities to the status of Special Assistance or as Centre of Advanced Study.

It has been accepted that a scholar must use the original sources and not mere translations. It is necessary to possess the knowledge of Sanskrit and/or Prakrit as well as some knowledge of scripts used in coins and inscriptions to do research work in Ancient Indian History. Similarly, one is required to know Urdu, Arabic and Persian to tap the sources in Medieval Indian History. But it is a sad fact that hardly five percent of scholars have the necessary competence to handle the sources in original in the above mentioned fields of research. This problem has to be tackled in all seriousness if we want to achieve the real purpose. So far, no concrete step has been taken in this direction.

It is heartening to note that the UGC conducted four workshops at Gauhati, Mysore, Amritsar and Baroda for history teaching in India perspectives and Programmes for the Eighties in 1976 which included discussion on M.Phil and Ph.D programmes in the universities. A consolidated report on these workshops on modernization of history courses in the Universities was published in 1978. The report lays down due emphasis on the language competence.[12]

It seems the universities in general have not been able to take care of this matter perhaps due to time lag or lack of resources. The problem can be sorted out at under-graduate level by proper planning of history teaching. Selected Colleges and Universities may be helped to start Honours Courses and encouraged to do the needful in the matter by providing additional staff and resources. The Colleges or the Universities which are already running Honours Courses should be instructed to follow this strictly. It is impracticable to teach a new language at research level. The old parrots study hard. It is a timely need to organize a few workshops and/or a national level workshop specially to reorient M.Phil and Ph.D programmes which may ultimately result in reshaping the Under-Graduate courses or planning them at that level if no practical solution is found out to tackle the problem at research level.

Role of Indian Council of Social Science Research, New Delhi

The Indian Council of Social Science Research (ICSSR) was established in 1969. It has undertaken a large programme of surveys of research in various social sciences. The prospectus of social sciences, as covered by the ICSSR includes the following disciplines:
1. Economics (including commerce), 2. Education, 3. Management (Including Business Administration), 4. Political Science (Including International Relation), 5. Psychology, 6. Public Administration, 7. Sociology (Including Criminology and social work).

The council is also concerned with the social science aspects of the disciplines of (1) Anthropology, (2) Demography, (3) Geography, (4) History, (5) Law, and (6) Linguistics.

The ICSSR has the taken a broad view of social sciences for the purpose of surveys, since developments in allied disciplines serve as inputs in social science research and also provide to it an inter-disciplinary perspective to which ICSSR is committed.

Historical studies containing social science aspects have always been considered to be within the purview of social sciences. This is so for the obvious reason, that, in the last three to four decades, historians have enlarged their interest from purely political history to its economic, social and cultural aspects that give meaning to researches in the broad field of social sciences.[13]

The Council has established a social science documentation centre at New Delhi and six regional centres at Bombay, Calcutta, Chandigarh, Delhi, Hyderabad and Shillong.

The Social Science Documentation Centre has been renamed in 1986 as National Social Science Documentation Centre (NASSDOC) at 35, Ferozshah Road, New Delhi – 110001. It compiles short bibliographies on demand from research scholars and other users on the topic of their interest[14].

Notes

1. R.C. Majumdar, *Historiography in Modern India,* Bombay, 1970, p. 37.
2. *Ibid.,* p. 38.

3. *Ibid.*
4. G. Kitson Clark, *Guide for Research Students Working on Historical Subjects,* OUP, 1972, p. 31.
5. As quoted by R.C. Majumdar, *op. cit.,* p. 39 from G.P. Gooch, *History and Historians of the Nineteenth Century,* 1913, p. 19.
6. R.C. Majumdar, *op. cit.,* p. 56.
7. R.P. Misra, *Research Methodology,* A Handbook, New Delhi, 1989, pp. 1-2.
8. Jadunath Sarkar in the *Foreword to the Vakataka-Gupta Age* by R.C. Majumdar and A.S.Altekar (Eds.), p. iv.
9. G.R. Elton, *The Practice of History,* London, 1967, p. 21.
10. *Ibid.,* p. 22.
11. The Proceedings are published by the United States Information Service, New Delhi under the title *American Studies in India.*
12. *History Teaching in India: Perspectives and Programmes for the Eighties,* pp. 106 - 107.
13. Foreword by G. Parthasarthi, Chairman, ICSSR to *Survey of Research in Economic and Social History of India* by R.S. Sharma (ed.), Ajanta Publications, Delhi, 1986.
14. Brochure Issued by Director NASSDOC New Delhi in February 1999.

3

AREA OF RESEARCH AND THE TOPIC

History is the study of the living past. We are not interested in the whole past one and the same time, some particular aspects of it merit attention from time to time and get the focus of historical research.[1] A scholar must get himself acquainted with the prospective areas of research. The scholar must review a broad area of his research interest along with his research guide before arriving at a research topic. It is not something which can be given in hand.

As somebody remarked in a lighter vein–It is far easier to suggest the selection of a spouse than a research topic.

Role of Research Scholar

It is the sole responsibility of the scholar to find his way to select a topic. To familiarise himself with the probable areas of current trends in research, he should consult Indian Council of Historical Research *News Letter* and *Indian Historical Review,* the Journal published by the Council which will acquaint him with the topics approved for fellowships and grants by the council and the reviews of the latest works published on the subject. Apart from that, he should consult other journals mentioned in Chapter II. He should consult the subject index of the University Library and take a broad view of the books on the subject he is interested to work. He should take out some of those books from the Library shelves and in particular go through the reverse of the title page and / or introduction where the basic information about the work, such as originally a thesis approved for the Degree of Philosophy of the University, the University name is given. This will apprise him about the scheme of chapterisation of works submitted for such degrees. He should also consult some issues of the *University News* and the *Bibliographical List of Dissertations on Humanities and Social Sciences,* published by the Association of Indian Universities, New Delhi. To get information about the noted works he should consult Maureen L. P. Patterson, *South Asian Civilizations,* A Bibliographical Synthesis, The University of Chicago Press, Chicago, 1981 and other Bibliographies available in the library, printed by the publishing houses.

After the scholar has familiarised himself with the above-mentioned works and feels himself somewhat equipped for thinking over an area of study, he should care for the guidelines provided in the Consolidated Report on the UGC Workshop on History courses which we quote here for the benefit of the readers.

The subjects for Ph.D dissertation may ordinarily be chosen from the following:

(a) "Dark areas i.e. problems of areas on which no or very little research has so far been done and fruitful research is possible and required;

(b) Problems and areas where limited research work has been done but which have scope for further investigation;

(c) Areas of social, economic and scientific history material culture including science and technology in India; social and economic formation processes in India covering all periods and all parts of India;

(d) Intellectual and cultural developments in India in different periods and different parts; history of ideas in all periods; and

(e) Critical editions of significant texts and documents, with due annotations and introduction bringing out the historical and related value of the work".[2]

We may comment that sometimes it may be more useful to take up a topic on which a lot of work has been done and if there is a scope for critical assessment and evaluation of different interpretations. But such a work needs a lot of patience and critical acumen of the scholar. Having done his homework along these guidelines, and deliberations on some topics in his area of research interest, the scholar should approach his supervisor for his opinion and discussion on the matter which may in due course of time culminate in the choice of subject.

Role of Supervisor

The supervisor plays, though a minor but a very vital and crucial role in the conduct of research by an amateur scholar. He has to provide guidelines to the young researcher, set his path more clearly and give him some insights from time to time. Otherwise it may be a useless adventure in many cases. The supervisor, before giving his consent to guide the subject must satisfy himself on the following points:

(i) that research on the proposed subject can be profitably pursued;

(ii) that the research work can be suitably undertaken at the University; and

(iii) that the candidate possesses the competence for the proposed research.

Further the supervisor himself must be interested in that area of study and investigation thereof; he should also be sure about his competence to guide the research. It should not be like a supervisor who when confronted on this issue in the Board of Studies Meeting in a University over a curious subject told us "Sir, I have no idea of the subject listed here but the student had told me that he will work on this subject and that too only under my guidance!".

The scholar, after finalizing his choice of subject, may prepare a rough bibliography on the subject so as to know the scope of his topic and ensure the availability of source material. This may be done on the advice and in consultation with the supervisor.

Planning at Research Level

Nowadays normally a research scholar is expected to write two dissertations – one for M.Phil degree and the other for Ph.D.

The M.Phil degree is quite often stated to be a terminating degree for those students who, due to lack of competence or for one reason or the other are unable to pursue higher research. In any case, the ideal will be that there should be a linkage between the two programmes, which is unfortunately lacking in most of the cases. The topic of research at M.Phil level, looking at its time duration of one year or a year and a half can be a micro-level study which may be pursued at Macro-level for Ph.D. degree. In a subject like history there is no dearth of subjects which is often shown and made a baffling problem. One may take up the study of an old village or Taluqa for M.Phil dissertation and a town or district for Ph.D. dissertation depending upon its rich potential. In other case, one may identify a town or district for M. Phil. and a province or region for Ph.D. programme. Sometimes a study of one or two villages or a temple/temples may suffice for the lower research degree and an area/region or a cluster of temples or monuments belonging to one or two religious sects may provide optimum results for a higher degree. The scholar and supervisor should together deliberate over such issues. The topics may concern socio-economic growth, place-name patterns, art and architecture based on area/region covering a suburb, town, capiṭal-town, port-town, city, metropolis or province or adjoining regions. The list can be added to any length. The scholar must clearly define his area of research in spatial and temporal terms.

The supervisor may vary a student who approaches him and just for saving appearances, make a stray reference to some topic which has already been worked or is being worked out in a neighbouring university. The supervisor must keep abreast of such information so as not to be misled and getting involved in unnecessary criticism.

A supervisor may identify a student while teaching him/her at post-graduate level with some area of research and test its feasibility at the level of research if the student comes to him by his/her own choice or allotted to him by the Department as the case my be. If a scholar having a post-graduate degree from some other university, approaches the supervisor, he may prescribe certain readings in the forms of books/articles and perceive the aptitude of the scholar before arriving at a decision for the choice of a subject.

Choice of a Supervisor

The relationship between the scholar and supervisor is very intimate and important. The research students are known as *Mānasa Putras* (Offsprings of mind) of the teacher. The student is a replica of the teacher in so many ways. By his close association as a research scholar, he emulates many traits of his teacher. A scholar is very lucky if he can find a guide who is a good scholar, with all his busy schedule and engagements remains accessible to his student and there is no communication gap between the two. The philosophy behind the research guidance is that a senior scholar who has several fertile ideas and is endowed with the capacity for opening up new vistas of research has little time to experiment with them due to his official engagements and other assignments as well as little physical capacity to involve himself in the collection of data and field work if required owing to his advancement in age. These two factors deter him to give practical shape to his imagination and ideas while a research scholar who is a novice in the field always needs his patronization and encouragement. Thus, a research work is a joint venture to a great extent.

The best way for the choice of a supervisor is by open system which means choice by the scholar himself/herself duly endorsed by the supervisor. As a matter of fact no research student should be thrust over the supervisor and *vice-versa*. That may give no chance for any dispute and is sure to bring out the best optimum results. The new mechanics of selection and allotment of research students by the Department has made it more or less mechanical by totally ignoring the human factor involved in it. This harm has been done on the name of systematisation of the admission procedure.

Most of the departments in the universities follow the allotment system whereby the research scholars, after they have joined the

Department are allotted to the respective teachers according to their area of specialization. Here the student has little say or no say at all. This has created innocuous situations at times. Even the open system in few departments is being replaced by allotment system. This is hampering genuine research interest at all levels.

There is a set rule for the number of research scholars which different categories of teachers i.e. Lecturers/Readers/Professors can guide. At times this rule is also flouted to the maximum. Not only that, some politics is also played in this allotment system which gives a further blow to research activity. The University administration remains quite indifferent to all this, till some serious problems crop up on the scene.

Systematization of admission procedure is better than the haphazard system which was followed earlier, provided the Head / Dean of the Department resists the temptation of controlling the choice of supervisor than leaving the faculty and scholars free for selection by mutual choice. This should be the ideal, by leaving a period of atleast three months to arrive at some decision by the teacher and the student. There is an old adage that "well begun is half-done". Only after testing this to the full extent, other procedures may be followed if need be. Under the old system of registration, we found most of the candidates got registered themselves under the supervision of the Head of the Department who had a big queue with him. This was done by the new aspirants keeping in view the convenience in paper work, approval of synopsis, recommendation for fellowship/scholarship, expectation of a job and smooth-sailing in achieving the final goal. Some politicians also registered themselves for the sake of prestige and easy access to the faculty and the students as it did not need a rigorous admission procedure. If the Head of the Department did not like a student for his consideration due to any reasons whatsoever, he sent them to other senior faculty who tested their suitability at a personal level to retain them or leave them. All said and done, the human element in joining the research activity was not missing, rather it was a focal point. Under the present system of admissions, this human element is largely missing which is not only desirable but essential in the matter.

The present system is rather more mechanised. We must strike a balance between the two if we want to achieve the goal of good research productivity.

It has been suggested that there may be an advisory committee of two or three faculty members, for guiding research, instead of a single guide.[3] It may be more suitable only for inter-disciplinary areas and problems.[4] In normal cases, it may do more harm than good by creating more problems for the research scholar than solving them.

Change of Supervisor

Once a supervisor has been fixed by self-choice of the scholar or by allotment by the Department, it should not be allowed to change for matters of discipline. If any system has to work, it should not be broken or pushed out of gear. Even under special circumstances, where a guide has been transferred or is on leave for longer duration, the name of the first guide should be retained even though another guide may be allotted with the proviso that any one of the guides will be permitted to forward the thesis for submission for the degree. However, it will be compulsory to inscribe the names of both the guides on the title page of the Thesis.

The role of a supervisor cannot be minimized. The guidance of research is as crucial in the initial stages as it is in the duration of work leading to the final goal. The mere absence of the supervisor due to leave or transfer should not be used as a pretext to snatch away the entire credit from him and impose it solely on somebody else to enrich his credentials. There are several cases of such exploitation in the universities. Even though it is ordained that any change of supervisor could only be accomplished with the consent of the supervisor. The change of supervisor has been effected arbitrarily under some such false pretext or the other by the Department/Board of Studies, the University administration playing a lukewarm or indifferent attitude in the matter. It becomes very much embarrassing on the part of student or teacher to react to the change. There are cases where the teachers have strongly reacted as the students were either misguided, lured or intimidated. On the other hand some teachers have tolerated this unpleasant change marred by silence. This kind of politics certainly provides disincentives to the research activity.

Role of Seminars

The students at research level should be encouraged to participate in Seminars / Conferences / Workshops organized at Local / Regional or National level. Some seminars could also be organized at departmental level or school level where the advanced research students / faculty could be requested to give some seminars in the areas of their research. This should be done on a voluntary basis. In case the seminars are thrust upon the research scholars or made compulsory, they may not be readily ripe to expose themselves before the faculty and the larger audience. Any disbursement of half-baked ideas or theories during the earlier stages of their research may become a laughing stock for others and any genuine criticism by others may discourage rather than encourage them by leaving them in cold blood while creating flames of hatred for those who criticised them even with a positive outlook. A research atmosphere of the sort should be created in the department. The young scholars, taking a cue from their seniors, offer themselves to give a seminar on their research topic or subject of their interest. They may be persuaded by offering them intensive painstaking research guidance on the material collected by them to give a seminar but should never be compelled to do so. The research activity should be made more pleasant and less cumbersome.

Difficulties Ahead

There may be problems ahead in the waiting, if some accidental obstructions involving the pains of a childbirth which are there when you intent upon doing on original and creative research work. It need not dishearten you if you notice in the midst of your work that somebody else is also working on the same or similar topic in the same area. You must ascertain whether you are duplicating another man's work, whether you can help each other or whether either of you are likely to get in each other's way.[5] This can be done either by meeting the person or corresponding with him/her on this issue. If you discover at a later stage that somebody has already worked on the subject which very closely resembles yours, there is no need to despair and take a momentous decision of change of intention. Nobody has a monopoly over research topics, you have as much right to research on the subject as anybody else. But you must find out whether his objectives and methods of treatment are different than yours.[6] You must modify and change a little bit if the need arises. To pre-empt all such possibilities, you should be on the regular look out of the bibliographies, journals, the newly published works and the book-reviews.

There may be a chance that your supervisor leaves you on transfer of his services on promotion or goes abroad for a year or two on some foreign assignment. There are possibilities of coming across a text which needs a translation for you or some work essential for your research is not available or you have collected material which has become unmanageable for you. You should not lose patience. Try to be faithful to your instincts and remain loyal to your supervisor. Some silver lining will come to your rescue in such cloudy weather. Your patience and loyalty may ultimately give you rich dividends.

Another difficulty you may come across is that when you want to change the title of your topic or delimit it from what you have registered with the University. There is a lurking fear in your mind that your thesis may get rejected on technical grounds or may not be forwarded by the Head of the Department / Dean of the School or may not be accepted by the Academic section of the University in case you change your topic. Some universities do not allow any change or modification and want you to follow every letter of the topic; while others allow the retitling of it even with some slight changes. As the work advances, the picture becomes more clear. Hence the scholar is within his rights to change or modify the title of his/her thesis. Normally the universities should allow the rectification of the topic with the permission of the supervisor six months before the submission of the thesis.

Notes

1. Om Prakash, "Perception of Social Reality and History" in Janak Pandey (Ed.) *Social Reality : Perspectives and Understanding*, New Delhi, 1988, pp. 115-116.
2. *History Teaching in India,* Perspectives and Programmes for the Eighties, UGC, 1978, p. 107.
3. *Ibid.*, p. 100.
4. *Ibid.*
5. Kitson Clark, *op. cit.*, p.16.
6. *Ibid.*

4

SYNOPSIS AND NOTE TAKING

Synopsis

You should be sure of yourself, your guide and your topic before you venture upon the detailed synopsis of your work. A good synopsis serves the purpose of a road-map or an atlas for your research journey. Before you draw out a plan for your research you must have a broad vision of your area / theme of study. You must know thoroughly what work has already been done in the field and you must know what you want to accomplish. You must raise certain questions and problems in the area, with an eye to resolve them. You must know the variations. You must take down notes on some sheet of paper lest you forget them. Some other questions / doubts will come to your mind during the course of your work. You must note them down simultaneously. You take care to discuss some of these ideas with your supervisor. You should proceed with caution and never be hasty in jumping at the conclusions. After you exchange your ideas with other colleagues and your supervisor, you will know their real worth. These questions should be put in the form of various hypotheses and not as firm connotations or as your findings till they are tested on the data available to you. Some of these may be even discarded if not found suitable on second thought or after discussion with other scholars or the supervisor.

Your synopsis should be tentative in the first instance. It should include a few words of introduction, containing a brief outline and research methodology to be followed by you. To lay down more clearly it should be prepared under the following headings:

(i) Title of the Topic

(ii) Importance of the Subject

(iii) Scheme of Chapterisation

(iv) Method and Approach

In case you are using more than one method of research e.g. historical method coupled with interview method, you may mention *Method / Methods and Approach* under the last heading.

You must show your synopsis to the supervisor, incorporate his suggestions. Now it is ready for submission as and when so required by the Department or University Administration.

Note Taking

We may state that synopsis-making and note taking have a very close relationship. While taking notes from various books and journals i.e. collecting data from the secondary sources you must take care of the scheme of chapterisation of your work. You should inscribe a heading over the card and underline it under the name of one of the chapters to which this material belongs. If it is related to more than one chapter, mention the other heading with an oblique and the third one within square brackets. It will be very easy for you to arrange your material and process it for a write-up.

A historian should work like a detective for his note-taking. American researchers first raise the question with an eye on the data and then collect their source material. European historians on the other hand first begin with the collection of the source material and then raise legitimate questions. While the Indian counterpart looks and works for both.[1]

Reprography has revolutionized the task of material collection. You should distinguish the material you need in full from a book or journal and get it xeroxed. While doing so, don't forget to include the name of the author, book, and the place and year of publication, edition ,etc for the book and the name of the journal, volume number and year of publication in case of the journal.

For collection of the rest of the material where note-taking is the only resort, you must have two types of cards–one for taking notes and the second one for bibliography. The first one should be 5" × 7" i.e. one-third of a foolscape paper and the second one– "3 × 5" i.e. post card size. You can get these cards on order from any stationery shop. As you start your work on the cards for collection of material, mention the name of the author (author's full name) as usual, the name of the book underlined, place and year of publication along with edition (edn.) on the top of the card. Taking down the matter, you should leave some margin on the left side of the card. The card possessing the material from an article from a book should first mention the name of the author mentioning the title of the article in quotation marks i.e. within inverted commas in the work cited in underline with the author's name within brackets, indicating (ed.) or (eds.) if it is more than one person. If there are more than two persons, you should state along with the name of the author, mentioning only the first author and others (or *et al.*) and lastly the page number or numbers as the case may be. If material from a journal is taken, it should indicate the name of the author, the title of the article in quotation marks, the volume of the journal and page numbers. Simultaneously, you must prepare a bibliographic card, indicating the name of the author by surname first, title of the book, place of publication and year of publication. Also take care to note the call number in the upper left hand corner mentioning the source i.e. the name of the library. This will help you to call for the book again in case you need it. Preparing the bibliographic card in alphabetical order will help you to arrange the final bibliography author-wise at the end. You can arrange and rearrange these cards subject-wise or for classification purposes. A few examples shall suffice:

Note Card (Basic Form)

(i) Gopal Krishan, *Spatial Dimensions of Unemployment and Underemployment,* New Delhi,1986, p., or pp.,.

There is no need to show the edition over and again, if you are using the same edition mentioned in the bibliography. For place of publication, only mention the first name even if ten names are given.

(ii) *Note Card* (Two authors): Bridget and Raymond Allchin, *The Rise of Civilization in India and Pakistan,* New Delhi, 1983, p., or pp.,.

(iii) *Note Card* (edited work by one author) Jim G. Shaffer, "Cultural Development in the Eastern Punjab", in Jerome Jacobson (ed.), *Studies in the Archaeology of India and Pakistan,* New Delhi, 1986, pp. 195-235.

(iv) *Note Card* (Edited by Two authors) B. K. Thapar, "Six Decades of Indus Studies" in B. B. Lal and S.P. Gupta, (eds.) *Frontiers of the Indus Civilization,* New Delhi, 1984, pp. 1-25.

(v) *Note Card* (Edited by more than three authors) B. K. Thapar, "The Aryans : A Reappraisal of the Problem" in L. Chandar, *et al.* (eds.) *India's Contribution to the World Thought and Culture,* Madras, 1970, pp 147-164.

(vi) *Note Card* (Article in a Journal) Peter Robb, "Ideas in Agrarian History : Some Observations on the British and Nineteenth Century Bihar" in *Journal of the Royal Asiatic Society* of Great *Britain and Ireland,* No. 1, 1990, pp. 17-43.

Bibliographic Card

Here surname of the author should come prior to the other part of the name. Thapar, Romila : *Ancient Indian Social History, Some Interpretations,* New Delhi, 1978, Reprinted, 1987,

You can write the classification No. and Accession No. of the Library along with its name on the space below or on the right side of the card.

Methods of Note-Taking

You can xerox the article from the journal or book or the relevant pages which you need the most. In case of note-taking on a card, after mentioning the particulars of the article, mention the page number if you are taking down a small excerpt out of it and take care to note down the changed page number as the case may be.

There are in general three methods of note-taking [2]:

(1) You may summarize the general idea of the large amounts of materials.

(2) You may paraphrase i.e. restate the material in your own words. That is when you do not need the exact writing but want detailed notes on specific sentences and passages.

(3) Transcribe the material exactly word for word, comma for comma. This is when you want to quote some sentence or passage in original to add lustre to your writing according to your judgement. While quoting, do not even change the spellings, quote verbatim.

Be careful in summarising or paraphrasing author's idea. Always strive for accuracy.

Notes

1. John C.B.Webster, *An Introduction to History,* Delhi, 1977, p. 30. Robin W. Winks (Ed.) *The Historian as Detective, Essays on Guidance,* New York, 1969, p. XXXI.
2. Joseph Gibaldi and Walter S. Achtert, *MLA Handbook for Writers of Research Papers.* New Delhi, Third Edn., 1989, p. 21.

5

SOURCE MATERIAL IN HISTORICAL RESEARCH

Importance of Source Material

Somebody was talking on the telephone to a friend when he said "Facts are facts whatever version you may give". True, some part of a story you cannot change while the other part you can change or twist. For example a dual fight took place between two adversaries, may be accepted beyond doubt·but who started first or who beat whom may be denied and has to be weighed upon other counts. Even though changed versions may be given in the second part, it can be ascertained on circumstantial evidence. Truth cannot be covered by falsehood, covering the blooming truth is like covering the fire by a piece of cloth which is impossible.

The facts are important for reconstruction of history which have to be based on evidence. Where from this evidence comes? It comes from the sources. You must know your sources intimately and prune them properly. Eye witnesses, complainant and defendants, documentary and/or living material can help us to know the truth. There is paucity of all evidence materially available for historical research. The heroes and villains of the event have vanished from the scene, eye-witnesses have also disappeared, only leaving some stray documentary evidence and living material at our disposal. Sometimes only part of evidence is available which we have to patiently discover or dig out the other part. That part of evidence is enough to awaken our curiosity to discover the rest of evidence to complete the story.

Many a time, the evidence in one form is not acceptable to us without the full form. The best example to quote about it is the historicity of Rāmagupta. From the inscriptional evidence of the Gupta inscriptions, Chandragupta II was regarded as the legitimate heir to the throne accepted by his father Samudragupta. The evidence of the identity of his elder brother Rāmagupta and the episode connected with him about surrendering his Chief Queen Dhruvadevī to the Śaka enemy, for the sake of peace treaty and thereafter Chandragupta taking up courage to disguise himself as the Chief Queen by killing the Śaka chief, appropriating the kingdom and Queen to himself, the evidence forthcoming from literary tradition was totally unacceptable, deemed to be a product of imagination only taken as a fabricated concoction. Even when the numismatic evidence came forth; it was dismissed, only accepting Ramagupta as a local ruler of Malwa. It was not till epigraphic evidence clinched the issue, with the epithet of Māhārājādhirājā (independent sovereign) for Rāmagupta that historians accepted, Rāmagupta as a shadowy figure of the Imperial Gupta family. That may also explain why his name was obliterated in the inscriptional lineage described in the inscriptions of the Imperial Guptas.[1]

Sometime even a last minute appearance of a new evidence may change the shape of things altogether, like in a Hindi movie, where a film hero is being taken by the police to be hanged to death as a consequence of the court verdict, when suddenly, somebody appears on the scene and makes confession of his crime. So the sources are the most important segment in history.

Verification of a Document or Text

Whenever you come across a document or text, the first and primary task for you is to ascertain its authorship, authenticity and date which we call external criticism. Having done that, you must look for the interpolations, factual errors in the original work and more carefully, if it is a translated text from the original work in some other language as also the annotations and interpretations by contemporary scholars and later commentators which we call as internal criticism of the document or text.

Let us review some of the problems with the sources, and the precautions to be kept in mind while using them for a historical reconstruction. Before we go into the specific sources, let us consider some general but major issues confronting a researcher.

Literature: General Issues

The first and foremost issue will be the Aryan problem *vis-a-vis* Vedic literature. Basically two divergent views have been expressed so far by scholars. One view is that the Aryans came from outside India soon after the decline of the Indus Valley Civilization i.e. around 1500 B.C. The other view is that they are indigenous. At present, the archaeologists have withdrawn their earlier most accepted theory of Aryan invasion for the destruction and decline of the Indus Valley Civilization. We all know that the Indus Civilization was urban civilization while the Vedic Civilization was pastoral-cum-rural civilization, initially. If the Aryans are indigenous, then according to the theory of socio-economic formations, the Vedic age should precede the Indus Valley Civilization. That would change the entire chronological sequence. If the Aryans and the Dravidians belong to the same indigenous stock, we will elicit a different kind of information than we do at present. The early Vedic Geography is limited to the area of 'Sapta Sandhu' i.e. the seven rivers – Satluj, Beas, Ravi, Chenab, Jhelam, Ganges and Yamuna – though Saraswati is also mentioned which seems to have changed its course or disappeared; on the other hand along with the Gangetic Doab, the Indus Valley Civilization seems to have covered the major portion of India–North-West, Punjab, Himachal, Haryana, Rajasthan, Gujarat, Maharashtra, etc. The technological improvement, extension and expansion can only be a later stage in human evolution. Surprisingly enough, the *Vedas* have been chronologically fixed by the Western and the West-oriented scholars later than the Indus Valley Civilization as 1500 B.C. This seems to be erroneous on another ground in the light of the present state of knowledge. We are obliged to S.R. Rao who has conducted Dwarka excavations and explorations with the science of oceanography and has pushed back the dating of the *Mahabharata* War to 1400 B.C. Hence the need to push back the Vedic Chronology.

The *Vedas* are stated to have come from the God and are not the works of human beings, "Apauraseya". Then how can we interpret the contemporary Vedic society on that count? Though it has been mentioned that the sages only perceived them "Rsyah mantra-drashaṭārah babhūvuḥ"–that can be true of all forms of knowledge. If we are not atheists, we can say that the Almighty is the originator, man is the doer. Historians have not ruled out the role of chance and divinity in human events.

Similarly, there is a different use of terminology for use of the *Vedas* as source materials by western and traditional scholars. The Western scholars use the term–Early Vedic Age to denote the Rigvedic age. On the other hand, the traditional scholars interpret the age of the three *Vedas* called 'Trayi' i.e. *Ṛgveda, Sāma Veda* and the *Yajur Veda* while taking the *Atharva Veda* and the Brahmanical literature for the Later Vedic Age. The Western Scholars consider the *Sama Veda, Yajur Veda* and the *Atharva Veda* for the study of the later Vedic Age. Thus there are problems of the authenticity ; chronology and terminology confronting us when we want to use the Vedic Literature for reconstruction of the history of the period. On face value also, the period of the Vedic Literature has been termed as *Proto-history,* until and unless there is supporting evidence and corroboration of the evidence from archaeological and other sources.

Sanskrit literature itself is classified into various forms – Kavya, Drama, Prose, Katha, Akhyayika, Lexical Literature, the Epics, the *Puranas,* the *Dharmasastras,* the Scientific literature, Rhetroics, Historical Kavya literature, poetics, so on and so forth. Not only that, the use of Sanskrit language in inscriptions and on coins forms another form of enormous literature. Each genre has its own technique, language and method – the entire information cannot be taken for granted and has to be sifted.

When we come down to the *smrtis* or the Dharmaśāstra literature we again know that the dates are tentative: As also is the case with regard to the date of the *Artha-Sastra* of Kautilya. Similarly, the dates of the epics themselves are a matter of controversy.[2] The matter of interpolations has been touched upon by some Western scholars but has never been dealt with scientifically. They may mention an interpolation, but when enquired into, they have nothing to say to prove it or disprove it usually. We should not admit it till we have any evidence supported by tradition. For example the view that the big epic 'The *Mahābhārata*' had seen three recensions 'Jaya', 'Bharata' and finally the *'Mahābhārata'* is also certified by information based on tradition.

The *Vedas* according to our traditional information though called "Śruti' have been brought to us very faithfully to each syllable and word by way of *'Pada-Paṭha', 'Krama-Paṭha', 'Jata-Paṭha'* and *'Ghana-Patha'*. Even then some foreign scholars and following them some others, opined that the II to VIII Mandal, as of the *Ṛgveda* are earlier while the IX, I and X are the later ones. We have no evidence to believe this. On the other hand, we know that the *Ṛgvedic* Aryans were the fire-worshippers and they worshipped the deity of Fire as the Messenger between the human beings and gods. The whole of the *Ṛgveda* is based on the praise of the gods through oblations given to them by fire. The first *ṛka* of the First Mandal starts with the praise and worship of the god of fire :

"Om Agnimīḍe Purohitam
Hotāram Ratnadhātamam"
" I praise Agni (the fire god) as she presents to the gods what valuable gifts we present to them through oblations".

We are again facing the same problems of variations in chronology, be it Kavya literature or the Dramaturgy, whether it is Mṛccha-kaṭika of Śudraka or works of Viśākhadatta or Bhāsa. We are on the horns of dilemma to use them as authentic sources for a particular period. Not even the date of Kalidasa, the poet-laureate of India, has been fixed up authentically – the scholars fixing his date in the First Century B.C., the Second Century A.D. or the Fourth Century A.D.

Seriously speaking, as a historian the whole plethora of information seems to be based on assumptions and presumptions. Then how can literature be used as a source material for the reconstruction of the past, which is uncertain and unknown. Still, there is a point in probing into the matter and carrying on the dialogue till we come to the surer grounds. Historian, like a detective never waits – starts his work with the cursory information, even unsure, and attempts to reach the truth as far as possible. He is always ready to consider with an open mind any new information, however, tacit, cursory and insignificant it may be. Apart from comparing the written authorities, there should be a checking of the written evidence by the use of non-literary evidence. This idea was impregnated in the cartesian historiography in the latter half of the seventeenth century that the testimony of written authorities must not be accepted without submitting into a process of criticism on the following principles (1) No authority must induce us to believe what we know cannot have happened, (2) The different authorities must be confronted with each other and harmonized, (3) The written authorities must be checked by the use of non-literary evidence.[3]

Buddhist Literature

Buddha himself is stated to have written nothing about his discourses. His teachings were communicated entirely by oral means. Where, when, and in what circumstances the thousands of the individual texts which Buddhism consists of, were first committed to writing remains in most cases unknown. It has been affirmed that the council literature came into existence over a period of roughly a thousand years, from the first to the tenth century of the Christian era. Even during the period of oral tradition, the complete words of the Buddha were referred to as the *Tripiṭaka,* the three 'baskets' or collections of the Buddha's words. These three are the *Vinaya Piṭaka,* the *Sūtra Piṭaka* and the *Abhidharma Piṭaka*. Together with the *Tantras,* they made up the four chief divisions of the canonical writings.[4]

The Vinaya Pītaka deals with "Conduct" i.e., the monastic discipline, the Sutra with the sermons of Buddha, literally meaning a thread, by extension of meaning the 'thread' of discourse connecting a number of topics, is perhaps the most important and characteristic of all Buddhist literary genres and the *Abhidharma*

Piṭaka meaning 'about Dharma' deals with metaphysics is a collection of highly scholastic treatises. The *Sūtra Piṭaka,* being the largest and most important is again divided into five groups (Nikāyas) namely (1) Digha (long) Nikāya, (2) Majjahima (Medium) Nikāya – shorter sermons, (3) Samyutta (connected) Nikāya, collections of brief pronouncements on kindred topics, (4) Anguttara (Graduated) Nikāya, a collection of over 2,000 brief statements, and (5) Khuddaka (Minor) Nikaya, miscellaneous works in prose and verse.

Among the contents of the khudaka are the *Dhanmapada* ("Verses on virtue"), the *Theragāthā* and the *Therigāthā*)"Hymns of the elder monks and Nuns"), which contain some of India's greatest religious poetry and the *Jātakas,* a collection of over 500 poems, briefly outlining folktales and other stories. The tales are told in full in a prose commentary attributed to Buddhaghosa, which is invariably published with the verses. Most of the tales are secular and are ascribed to the Buddha, who is said to have told them as recollections of his previous births as a *Bodhisattva,* being destined to become Buddha. These racy and vivid stories are great as literature and are an invaluable source of social history.[5] The Ajanta Paintings with its symbolism depicting the Jataka tales are now-a-days being interpreted as the most communicative art form of the period convincing the layman as to why he should follow Buddhism.

Apart from the canon and its many commentaries, we know about Buddhism from *Milinda–Panha* "Questions of Menander" an account of the discussions of the Greco-Bactrian king and the monk Nagasena–which is deemed as a semi–canonical work. We also know about Buddhism from the two Ceylonese chronicles *Dipavamsa* and the *Mahavamsa* (4th-5th century A.D.) which tell the history of Buddhism in Ceylon and give valuable information on political and social history also. The Mahavamsa was continued as the Cūlavaṁsa ("Lesser Chronicle") by a succession of monks down to the fall of kingdom of Kandy to the British at the beginning of the 19th century.[6]

Jain Literature

The origins of Jainism go back to prehistoric times. According to

Jainism, twenty-four *Tīrthankaras* or leaders of the religion flourished, the first being Rishabha, the twenty-second Nemi or Neminatha, the twenty – third Pārśva, Mahāvīra being the last one. The parents of Mahāvīra followed the creed of Pārśva. Mahāvīra was a senior contemporary of Buddha.[7]

Vardhamāna, known to his followers as Mahāvīra ("The great hero") founded Jainism, the "Religion of the Conquerors" *(Jinas)*. The Jain canon is preserved in twelve *Aṅgas* or sections, which replaced the fourteen "former texts" *(Purvas)*, while new material has been added to the original canon in the form of the twelve *Upāṅgas* or minor sections, and various lesser works.[8] Jain epistemological theory of relativity is well preserved in the doctrines of *syādvāda* and *nayavāda*.[9]

Vernacular Literature

From the 8th century onwards, there was a new trend in the political history of India i.e. the rise of regional states in Northern India, giving rise and popularity of the regional languages; the South in the ascendant and the crystallization of Tamil Culture.[10] This trend is also seen in the inscriptions–later inscriptions become bilingual employing Sanskrit generally at the beginning and the end, and the local speech of the people – Kannada, Telugu or Tamil – in the body of the document, particularly in the detailed description of gifts made and the boundaries of land given to temples, learned men and so on. From about the 10th century A.D. inscriptions being composed altogether in the popular speech became very common, though Sanskrit continued to the employed wholly or in part in the records and held an honoured place everywhere as the best medium of cultural intercourse.[11]

All the modern languages of India have had substantial literatures of their own, ranging over a period of 500 to 1,000 years, and in the case of three Dravidian languages, Tamil, Kannada and Telugu, even longer. Tamil, in particular, has a literary history older than any of the European languages, save classical Greek and Latin. Its earliest extant grammar *Tolkappiyam* (5th century A.D.), even the extant Sangam poetry, later collected in anthologies known as the *Ettutogai* (2nd – 3rd centuries A.D.), the famous *Kural,* known as the Veda of the Tamils, (6th century); and the *kavyas* or epics *Manimeghalai* and *Silappadigaram* in the 9th century A.D. This literature is more secular than religious. However, from 6th century onwards, we find the devotional poetry of the Saiva and Vaishnava saints, known respectively as the Nayanars and the Alvars, and culminating in the superb classic, the *Rāmāyaṇa* of Kamban in the 9th century, Kannada and Telugu, along with Malayalam, are permeated with Sanskrit heritage and have taken freely from its vocabulary. A new genre known as Champu, a mixed form of verse and prose, also familiar in Sanskrit, was perfected by the Kannada and Telugu poets from the 10th to the 13th centuries. From 10th to 12th centuries, three gems of Kannada literature namely Pampa, Ponna, and Ranna wrote in Champu style. The Telugu poets, Nannaya of the 11th century and Tikanna of the thirteenth also employed this form in their famous renderings of the *Mahābhārata.* In the middle of the 12th century, a popular religious movement, known as *Virasaivism,* swept over Karnataka (the Kannada–speaking area) and later over Andhra. The founder of the movement, Basava, and his followers retained their teachings in a simple unadorned prose, and their works, known as *vacanas,* are a landmark in medieval Kannada literature. The rise of Vijaynagara Empire in the 14th century gave further impetus to Kannada and Telugu literatures as well as the revival of Hindu Sanskrit tradition and it stood as a bulwark against the further Muslim encroachment on the South for more than two centuries. The Vijayanagara Empire achieved its highest glory in the 16th century under Krishnadeva Raya who was himself a poet both in Telugu and Sanskrit.[12] Similarly, the didactic verses of the Telugu poet Vemana in the seventeenth century or earlier and musical compositions of Tyagaraja in the eighteenth century are admired all over South India. Malayalam is the youngest of Dravidian languages, and although some songs and ballads of an earlier age have survived in oral tradition and some written texts take us back to the 14th – 15th centuries, the language established its full identity and distinctive quality only in the 16th – 17th centuries, namely through translations of the Sanskrit epic by the gifted poet Ezhuttachan. Despite its Dravidian origin, the literary development of Malayalam has been mainly under Sanskrit influence.[13]

As regards the languages of the North India, derived from the spoken dialects of Middle Indo-Aryan, their separate identities were perhaps not established till after the 11th century, for their earliest extant literary classics are not older than the 12th – 13th centuries. We may mention the Rajasthani classic Prithviraja Rasau (12th century) by Chand Bardai, Amir Khusrau (13th – 14th century) and Marathi Poet Jnanesvara's commentary on the *Bhagavad-Gita* (13th century). Similarly, we may mention of the works by Suradasa, Tulasidasa, and Mira Bai. Hindi was also known as Khari Boli, based on the Western Indo-Aryan dialect spoken in Delhi and its neighbourhood. The same language, when written in Perso-Arabic script, has evolved an identity of its own known as Urdu, literally from the original Turkish word 'Ordu' meaning an army or camp. Its first standardized literary form, known as *Dakhni*, was developed in the 15th century in Central and South India, where Muslim adventurers had carved out powerful kingdoms for themselves. This literary medium travelled back to the North, where the patronage of the Mughals, and later of the Lucknow court and society, it developed as a furnished product. It is worth mentioning that the best known of modern Hindi writers, Premchand, wrote his first stories and novels in Urdu and later turned them into Hindi.[14]

In the same way, in the 15th – 16th Centuries, the modern Indo-Aryan languages had their richest literary flowering, due to revival of interest in the Sanskrit language and the upsurge of Vaishnava *bhakti* which had an earlier literary sprouting in Tamil, in the poetry of Saint–Poets of the 6th century onwards. Its Philosophy, as expounded by the Tamil sage Ramanujaacharya was carried to North India in the 14th Century by Ramananda, who was traditionally the teacher of the famous poet Kabir. Madhavacharya from Karnataka carried *Bhakti* where its Bengali exponent was Bengali Saint Chaitanya, whose teachings spread from Orissa in the east to Vrindavan (near Mathura) in the west and travelling south had a marked influence on the development of Vaishnava poetry in Kannada–"a significant example of the cultural interaction of Dravidian and Indo-Aryan influences". To this may be added the general impact of Islam, the non-conformist Sufi tradition and the gradual infiltration of Perso-Arabic vocabulary and literary lore. The poems of Haba Khatun in Kashmiri, Bulley Shah, and Waris Shah in Punjabi and Shah Latif in Sindhi are landmarks in these literatures. These two Punjabi poets of the 18th century and their Sindhi contemporary wrote their lyrics round the tragic love tales of Hira and Ranjha, Sassi and Punnu, and Sohni-Mahival.[15] Apart from this we get Assamese *Buranjis* (court chronicles) and the later historical records in Marathi and Urdu; Rajasthani *khyats* and bardic literature, and historical accounts in the Gujarati, Bengali and Punjabi languages.[16]

Similarly, we have a plethora of materials in foreign accounts and chronicles from ancient to modern periods of Indian history.[17]

Apart from that, we have Archival sources. The National Archives of India at New Delhi offers source material on varied aspects of Indian history for the past two centuries. It maintains not only the commercial transactions of the East India Company in the 18th century but also abundant material on the growth of the British dominions.[18] The archives of the states are as valuable for the history of India as the records of the Union Government. The archives of judicial courts constitute another class of valuable source material for Indian history. Then there are private archives maintained by individuals, and families of note, the universities and educational institutions, banks, business houses and chambers of commerce. The history of India's struggle for independence can be enriched by the use of the papers of eminent leaders of the nationalist movement and records of organizations like the Indian National Congress which are available at the Nehru Memorial Museum and Library, New Delhi as well as the archival sources available abroad viz., Pakistan and United Kingdom at the India office Records (Commonwealth Relations office, London) are very useful.[19]

For the modern period, we have manifold sources of history in English language, French, Portuguese, German, Russian and etc., apart from more than twenty languages of India. English had the historical advantage of coming to India at a time when 'Sanskrit and Persian' had long played out their roles as languages of enlightenment and had become mere custodians of past glory and refuges of orthodoxy.[20] The modern literature of India is influenced by English, American and Russian literature apart from the old heritage of Sanskrit. The great thinkers like Rabindranath Tagore, Sri Aurobindo, Gandhi, Marx and Freud have also made their impact on it.[21]

Archaeology

Archaeology is a very important source of history. It adds scientific tinge to history. By archaeology, we mean first exploring a site of human habitat, then excavating it and identification of the patterns of culture. Archaeological evidence is a non-literary evidence which helps us to ascertain how much literary evidence is authentic. Thus it determines the extent of facts in history based on literary sources. It helps to sift the grain from the chaff or the husk of myth in history. Nowadays, archaeology as a source, is used for all periods of history. Recently, B. R. Mani is excavating the site of Lalkot in Delhi to dig out the material culture from Rajput period to Khilji period.[22] This technique is broadly known as historical archaeology. To quote from R. N. Mehta, "Archaeology in relation to written documents is not only known as historic archaeology but its operation on different time scales of written history gives it the name of Historic Archaeology, Medieval Archaeology, Industrial Archaeology, etc. Often techniques of archaeology are applied to specific literary work and the terms Biblical Archaeology, Puranic Archaeology and the like are used to indicate these features. When folk literature, oral tradition etc. are interpreted with the help of archaeology, the subject could be explained as Folk Archaeology. In these activities, the work or the traditions are viewed by the theory and practice of archaeology.[23]

Archaeology by itself is emerging as a full-fledged discipline. Now, we even hear about the Aerial Archaeology and Marine Archaeology. A few recent important works on methodology deserve our notice viz:

1. Walter Shepherd, *Archaeology,* New York, 1966.
2. David L. Clarke, *Analytical Archaeology,* London, 1968, Revised Edition, 1978.
3. Keith Branigan, *Archaeology Explained,* London, 1973, 1988.
4. Charles L. Redman and others (Eds), *Social Archaeology,* Beyond Substance and Dating, New York, 1978.
5. Keith Muckelroy, *Maritime Archaeology,* CUP, London, 1978.
6. S. J. Knudson, *Culture in Retrospect: An Introduction to Archaeology,* Chicago, 1978.
7. Clive Orton, *Mathematics in Archaeology,* CUP, 1980, paperback, 1982.
8. Myra Shacklay, *Environmental Archaeology,* London, 1981.
9. Fred Wendorf and Angela E. Clora (Eds.), *Advances in World Archaeology,* Vol. I, New York, 1982, Vol. 2, 1983, and Vol. 3, 1984.
10. Karl W. Butzer, *Archaeology as Human Ecology: Method and theory for a contextual approach*, CUP, 1982, Reprinted, 1984,1985.
11. Lewis R. Binford, *Working at Archaeology,* New York, 1983.
12. P. M. Masters and N.C. Flemming, *Quarternary Coastlines and Marine Archaeology: Towards the prehistory of land bridges and continental shelves,* London, 1983.
13. James A. Moore and Arthur S. Keene (Eds.) *Archaeological Hammers and Theories,* New York, 1983.
14. Mark S. Aldenderfer (Ed.) *Quantitative Research in Archaeology: Progress and Prospects,* California, 1987.
15. Michael Shanks and Christopher Tilley, *Reconstructing Archaeology : Theory and Practice,* CUP, 1987.
16. Lewis R. Binford, *Debating Archaeology,* California, 1989.

17. Colin Renfrew and Paul Bahn, *Archaeology: Theories, Methods and Practice,* London, 1991.

Archaeology has changed the face of Indian history by the discovery of the Indus Valley Civilization since 1922, continued by further exploration and excavation of hundreds of important sites since India became a free nation. A further breakthrough is expected by the efforts of well-known marine archaeologist Prof. S. R. Rao whose excavations at Dwarka have reasonably pushed back the date of the *Mahabharata* War by about half a century i.e. 1400 B.C., which by corollary is bound to push back the usually accepted dates of the Vedic Age. It may thus help us to arrive at better chronological tables.

Archaeology has, as a matter of fact, created many sub-disciplines, which deal with the variety of artefacts such as pottery, coins, inscriptions, monuments, food, dress, objects of worship, tools and implements, etc.[24] Some of them have emerged as separate disciplines by themselves as a matter of course. We shall deal with them one by one as far as their authenticity as a source of evidence for the reconstruction of the history of a period is concerned.

Pottery

Pottery craft developed with the emergence of the Neolithic cultures. However, in the Ganga Valley-Vidhyan plateau, pottery was known to the people since the Mesolithic period. At the earlier stages, the pottery was hand made, ill fired and of coarse fabric.[25]

Different varieties of pottery have been excavated from various parts of India. Of these four types are of cardinal importance. (1) Painted Grey Ware (PG Ware), (2) Northern Black Polished Ware (NBP Ware), (3) Rouletted Ware, (4) Black and Red Ware (also loosely called Megalithic Pottery). These types of ware are well known in archaeology and are of special chronological importance. The PG ware belongs to the Bronze Age, the NBP ware belongs to the Iron Age, and the Rouletted Ware is dated somewhere in the early decades of the 1st Century A.D., associated with Roman trade in South India. The distribution pattern of each of these ceramic groups suggests a particular area of focus though, with more or less overlapping boundaries.[26] The significance of these different pottery groups and their distribution has been conjectured by archaeologists, specially in terms of the process of cultural diffusion. But archaeologists have not differentiated between pottery making and pottery using cultures.[27]

Attempts have been made though on a speculative basis due to paucity of archaeological evidence to correlate Puranic lineages and archaeological cultures.[28] The Ochre Colour Pottery (OCP) occurred during the Harappan period, is at various sites succeeded by PGW culture; though at some other sites in Magadha, BRW (Black and Red Ware) is known, PGW is absent. It may be noted that BRW unlike PGW has an earlier start i.e. in 2000 B.C. and in some of the sites in Saurashtra and Kutch is associated with the late Harappan[29]. It will be more fruitful to have such an exercise of finding correlation with the historical tradition, once the archaeological picture is more clearly defined.

We cannot ignore the evidence that the PGW sherds have been found in the same areas as represented by the later Vedic texts. Although the PGW wares have been noticed in eastern UP and even in Bihar, their epicentre seems to be upper Ganga and Sutlej basins. However, there is nothing like an exclusive PGW culture because other wares such as black and red ware, black-slipped ware, red ware, and plain grey ware are also associated with them.[30] The material equipment of the PGW culture tallies with the later Vedic texts. We notice the beginnings of territorial state formation, advent of social stratification and the emergence of administrative machinery, in the later Vedic texts; all of them pre-suppose a full-fledged agrarian society, not typical of the Ṛgvedic phase. Although a good portion of the geographical areas covered by the *Ṛgveda* overlaps the area covered by the later vedic texts and PGW culture, the fact that Ṛgvedic people were mostly pastoral, used neither iron nor glass and cultivated only barley, rules out the possibility of their being equated with the memebrs of the PGW cultures.[31] Sinha has rightly emphasised the need for attempting at a history of ceramic technology in India to determine the pottery forms, shapes and sizes, the relationship with the development in metallurgy and ceramics, foreign influence on Indian pottery or foreign intrusion in the Indian scene, the relationship between the Central and North Indian Black and Red Ware and the Megalithic Ware of South India, the great gap in time sequence etc.,. [32]

Coins

The coins are a very important source of history, especially in India which did not produce in early times Herodotus or Thucydides, a Livy or Tacitus.[33] We could not have known about the Bactrian rulers in Punjab (200-100 B.C) and like wise the Scythian and Parthian invaders without the discovery of their coins.[34] Similarly, they are a major source of our knowledge about the various tribal and city republics and monarchical states that flourished in India during the pre-Christian centuries and thereafter. The coins often offer the names of persons or institutions that were responsible for issuing them. Of them, only some are known from epigraphic and literary records. By studying the coin types and their distribution we may be able to know the areas of rule of successive kings of the dynasty. We know about the kinds of metals used for composing the coins such as gold, silver[35], nickel (called 'White Iron' by the Greeks), the mixed metal such as Potin[36] and lead. By knowing the weight standards, we can identify their place in the currency system. The loss of weight may be accounted for debasement, forgery and fakeness by private hands and merchants. Even the epigraphical and Puranic data of the known dynasties such as the Satavahanas[37] or the Guptas[38] is corroborated, corrected and supplemented only by their coins. By studying the species of the coins in the hoards and the stratified evidence of coins, we may arrive at interesting pieces of information. The Bayana hoard is the biggest hoard of Gupta gold coins that has ever been recovered. Even after melting down of about 300 coins of the hoard, a total of 1821 coins could be recovered by the police.[39] It discloses a number of types and varieties of coins that were so far unknown e.g. the unique *Chakravikrama* type which shows Chandragupta II directly receiving a *Prasada* from Lord Vishnu.[40] Similarly, the various details of the motifs on the *Aśvamedha* type of coins of Samudragupta have been fully brought out than was so far done in earlier works.[41]

Coins also help us to know the social, religious and economic history of the people. They reflect on the idea about the workmanship, artistic excellence and aesthetic tastes of the people of those times. From the coins, we know about the popular religious cults and iconographic forms e.g. the Kushana Coinage depicts the Greek, Iranian, Buddhist and Brahmanical gods and goddesses, especially the Buddha in human form and Lord Shiva with four hands for the first time.[42] The Gupta coinage shows Indianisation of coins with Lakshmi sitting on a lotus, holding a lotus and scattering coins as Goddess of Wealth, in comparison to her original counterpart Ardoksho, known on the Kushana coins. We also find the figures of Durga, Ganga and Lakshmi on the coins of the Guptas.[43] The coins also throw light on the economic history of the period. We can study the weights and metrology of the coins, which are an indication of economic prosperity or decline of the people. D.D. Kosambi has made some pioneering efforts in the field and given scientific treatment to the subject. Some of the important articles are published by the Indian Council of Historical Research, New Delhi under the title *Indian Numismatics,* which merit the attention of the reader.

1. *A Statistical Study of the Weights of Old Indian Punch-marked Coins* pp. 1-6.
2. *On the Study and Metrology of Silver Punchmarked Coins*, pp.14-84.
3. *On the Origin and Development of Silver Coinage in India,* pp. 85-94.
4. *Scientific Numismatics*, pp. 145-156.[44]

Attempts have been made even to study the tribes and settlement patterns on the basis of coins and seals.[45] We have also inscriptions on coins and seals but they will come under the domain of numismatics. Such inscriptions give us a good deal of information about the nature of the tribe or personal qualities of a king.[46] With a discovery of a few coins, one should not jump to the conclusion of a ruler or dynasty in the area until and unless corroborated by other evidence. They may have been brought out by a trader or in terms of a transaction in the area.

The importance of coins for the study of any period of Indian history is now widely recognised.[47]

Epigraphy

It is with epigraphy, that is the discovery of inscriptions in fourth century B.C. we come to the domain of history. When the decipherment of the Indus Valley seals is reliably done, we can talk about the Indus Valley Civilization as the first beginning of history.

Inscriptions provide us the most authentic data and are more reliable than tradition and literature. They are the life-blood of history.[48] They regulate everything that we learn from tradition, literature, coins, art, architecture or any other source. In the absence of ancient historical compilations in India, they are a vital source of information. They are inscribed on metals such as iron, gold and silver, brass, bronze, copper and often authenticated by attaching a copper or bronze reproduction of the royal seal. The inscriptions on other substances than metal are found on crystal; on clay, on terra-cotta, on burnt brick, on earthenware and on stone in various forms, and even on rocks, columns and pillars, on carpets, on facades, walls and other parts of caves, images and statues and even on moulds for making seals. They may furnish us with information on plain statements of events, religious motives, religious endowments, secular donations, geography and royal genealogies.

The inscriptions were of no use to us until James Prinsap deciphered the Brahmi script in 1837 on the analogy of the Kharosthi and Greek inscriptions. From the Asokan inscriptions, we know about his concept of *Dharma,* polity and administration. The Thirteenth Rock Edict informs us about the Kalinga War and his resolve to renounce the policy of warfare.

We have the numerous inscriptional records available in various scripts, the Indus Valley script, Brahmi, Kharosthi, Nagari or Devanagari, Persian, Arabic and in the regional languages from the ancient period onwards to the contemporary period which throw a flood of light on various aspects of Indian history through the ages.[49]

Art and Architecture

As a matter of fact, a historian cannot ignore any form of art and architecture to have a full knowledge of any period of history, be it in the form of a building, temple, stupa, Mosque, Church or even a deserted site (which may reveal the lay-out or plan of the settlement or pattern of settlement), painting, sculpture and terracotta art. We can know about the town planning, country planning, structure, iconography, social life, economic life, religion, symbolism aesthetics, building materials, engineering skills, leisure and pastime, political changes and even foreign influences. We have a very vast heritage in the form of art and architecture surviving in India and various other countries of the world.[50]

Notes

1. T. R. Sharma, *A Political History of Imperial Guptas.* New Delhi, 1989, pp. 105-139.
2. For Classical Literature see A.K. Warder : "Classical Literature" in A.L. Basham (Ed.), *A Cultural History of India,* OUP, Delhi , 1975 Tenth Impression 1966 pp 170-192; A.L. Basham, *Wonder that was India,* Bombay, 1963 pp 386 – 452.
3. R.G.Collingwood, *The Idea of History* pp.61-62.
4. Bhikshu Sangharakshita, "Buddhism" in A.L. Basham (ed.). A *Cultural History of India,*_ Delhi, 1996 edn. pp. 88-89.
5. A.L. Basham, *The Wonder that was India,* Delhi, 1963 p267 and p. 453, ff.
6. *Ibid;* pp. 267-268.
7. A.N. Upadhya, "Jainism" in A.L. Basham(ed.), *A Cultural History of India,* pp. 100-101.
8. A.L. Basham, *The Wonder that was India,* pp 287-289.
9. *Ibid;* pp. 502-503.
10. Romila Thapar, *A History of India,* Volume I, Pelican, 1966, reprinted 1982, pp. 194 - 265.
11. K.A. Nilakanta Sastri, *A History of South India,* OUP, Bombay, Third edition, 1966, Second impression 1971, p.14.
12 Krishna Kriplani, "Medieval Indian Literature" in A.L. Basham (Ed). *A*

Cultural History of India, pp. 303-305; K.A. Nilakanta Sastri, *A History of South India,* pp. 1-33.

13. Krishna Kripalani, *op. cit.*, p. 305.
14. *Ibid.*, p. 307.
15. *Ibid.*, pp. 307-309.
16. *Ibid.*,. pp. 308-09; P.N. Chopra (ed.) *The Gazetteer of India,* Vol. 2, Publications Division, Government of India, New Delhi, 1973 pp. LVII-LX.
17. P.N. Chopra, *op. cit.* pp. LX-LXVIII.
18. *Ibid.*, pp. LXVIII-LXXI
19. *Ibid.*, pp. LXXI-LXXVII
20. Krishna Kripaloni, "Modern literature" in A.L. Basham (ed) *A Cultural History of India* p. 407
21. *Ibid.*, pp. 408-422.
22. *Tana–Bana,* T.V. Serial, 6.6.92.
23. R.N. Mehta, *Medieval Archaeology,* Delhi, 1979, Introduction, p.1.
24. Romila Thapar, "The Historian and Archaelogical Data" in Romila Thapar, *Ancient Indian Social History,* pp. 193-210.
25. Shashi Ashtana, *Pre-Harappan Cultures of India and the Borderlands,* New Delhi, 1985, pp. 244-252.
26. Baidyanath Saraswati, *Pottery-Making Cultures and Indian_Civilizaiton,* New Delhi, 1978, p.102.
27. *Ibid.*
28. Romila Thapar, "Puranic Lineages and Archaelogical Cultures" in Romila Thapar, *Ancient Indian Social History,* New Delhi, 1978, Reprinted 1987, pp.240-267.
29. *Ibid.*, B.P. Sinha (Ed) *Potteries of Ancient India,* Patna, 1970, Passim.
30. R.S. Sharma, "The Later Vedic Phase and the Painted Grey Ware, Culture" in Debiprasad Chattopadhyaya (Ed.) *History and Society,* Calcutta, 1978, pp.133-134
31. *Ibid.*
32. B.P. Sinha, "Some Problems of Ancient Indian Potteries" in B.P.Sinha, *Archaeology and Art of India,* Delhi, 1979, pp.31-33.
33. D.C. Sircar, *Studies in Indian Coins* , Delhi,_ 1968, p.1.
34. PL. Gupta, *Coins,* New Delhi, 1969, p. VII.
35. D.R. Bhandarkar, *Lecturers on Ancient Indian Numismatics,* 1921, Reprinted, Patna, 1984, p.140.

36. *Ibid.*, p. 145. An alloy which is composed of yellow and red copper, lead, tin and some dross. According to the varying proportions of its first two ingredients they look sometimes like bronze and sometimes like lead. Again billon is to silver what potin is to bronze. And potin coinage was struck along with lead coinage.
37. Mala Dutta, *A Study of the Satavahana Coinage,* New Delhi, 1990, Passim,
38. T.R. Sharma, *A Political History of the Imperial Guptas,* Delhi, 1989, Passim,
39. A.S. Altekar, *The Gupta Gold Coins in the Bayana Hoard,* Bombay, 1954, *Preface,* p.28; see also D.C. Sircar, *Studies in Indian Coins for discovery of numerous hoards,* pp. 304-312.
40. *Ibid.*, p.29.
41. *Ibid.*, p. 31.
42. P. L. Gupta, *Coins,* p. VIII.
43. *Ibid.*, pp. VIII-IX.
44. D.D. Kosambi, *Indian Numismatics,* New Delhi, 1981.
45. P. Gupta, *Geography from Ancient Indian Coins and Seals,* New Delhi, 1989; M.K. Sharan, *Tribal Coins: A Study,* Delhi, 1972.
46. M.K. Sharan, *op. cit., Passim,* A.S. Altekar, *op. cit., Passim.*
47. P.N. Chopra, *The Gazetteer of India*, Vol. 2 pp. XXXI-XLI.
48. *Ibid.*, p. XXI.
49. *Ibid.* pp. XX-XXXI.
50. P.S. Rawson, "Early Art and Architecture" in A.L.Basham (ed.), *A Cultural History of India,* pp. 197-211 and Martin S. Briggs, "Muslim Architecture in India" in A.L. Basham (ed.), *op. cit.,* pp. 310-325.

6

HISTORICAL METHOD

Attributes of a Historian

A social scientist is expected to understand the past in order to know the present properly and thus have the ability to predict or plan the future.

"The understanding of the past is not so easy as it is sometimes made to appear."[1] We are even unable to know quite often what is happening around us. Then how difficult it can be to know about the past which is shrouded in mystery. Historical truth, ancient or recent, is always complex and always difficult to ascertain. A historian is not only required to be a voracious reader but also needs to show keen interest in all other branches of knowledge as history is all-pervasive. A historian ought to know something about other social sciences such as Economics, Geography, Sociology, Political Science, Psychology, Anthropology, Philosophical systems and hence be acquainted with all unpredictable matters that human lives contain. At least, he should be ready to use the results supplied by others in their studies (called monographs) upon the related topics that he encounters while pursuing his own.[2] Hofstadter remarks in this connection as follows: "But to me it is not the formal methods of the social sciences, useful as they may be, that are of central significance but rather their substantive findings, their intellectual concerns, and their professional perspectives. Taken in this way, their value paradoxically rests not in their ability to open new methods to bear upon old problems, but in their ability to open new problems which the historian has usually ignored. Prompted by the social sciences, the historian begins to realize that matters of central concern to other disciplines force him to enlarge his conception of his task. Questions associated with social status, social mobility, differences and conflicts between generations, child-rearing in relation to its culture, the sociology of knowledge and of the professions, are questions which he might properly take upon himself, and which are interwoven with his traditional concerns."[3] This shows that the historian must be prepared to have a good grasp of the findings of the other related disciplines and the connected issues on the subject. This renews his task and also makes it difficult.

Thus history needs to be interpreted again and again in the light of new evidence, changing attitudes and norms.

This underlying need for "interpretation" differentiates history from the exact sciences. "Scientists who are accustomed to getting their results from controlled experiments in the laboratory find it difficult to understand why on the basis of apparently identical information, historians should form such divergent opinions. But this is simply because unlike scientists, historians deal with events that have passed, and they have thus no means of verifying reports made of them by organizing a repeat experiment. More, since report of past events come from observers whose narration must always be greatly influenced by their own biases,...."[4]–points out Prof. Irfan Habib. We may point out that it is not only the bias of the contemporary observer or author like Abul Fazal who views the reign of Akbar, the Great, differently than that as viewed by Badauni,[5] but how the reader or present day authors, who on the same available material, take different views on the same event of 1857 in India viz., characterizing it as a "Revolution" or a "Mutiny" or Nationalistic Struggle[6] which McCullagh alludes to cultural relativism.[7] That is why the facts of history do not close down with one historian as has been pointed out by Carr[8] but the interaction continues further between the historian and his reader, as had been pointed out by us in our earlier work : *The Concept of History.*[9]

The historian is obliged to answer six Ws in describing any happening, which is as follows :

1. What happened?
2. Where did it happen?

3. When did it happen?
4. To whom did it happen?
5. Why did it happen?
6. Who did it all, and how?

The doctrine of New Historicism applies the same yard-stick of cultural relativism even to see the events, as the products of several specific local social and cultural forces under which the people involved, acted as they did. In other words, the meaning of texts which people have produced in the past must be understood in relation to their social setting. However, we may believe that they can refer to the author's beliefs about society rather than society itself. The problem is that all this inevitably applies to the text of the historian as well. The disruptions of the past, with certain preferences, bias or unfairness, can still help us to know the truth about the past.[10]

On the other hand, a historian needs to be a specialist in a particular field in which he may be known such as Theatre historian, Art historian, Economic historian, Cricket historian and the like for which he is expected to have a thorough knowledge about the theories and practice in his respective area of specialisation. Here, he may like to adopt an inter-disciplinary approach but still historical perspective in the area is most important, apart from the quantifying techniques and statistical method which he may apply to gain his results by using a comparative approach. Another attribute which a historian should have is imagination which he needs to use in building up various hypotheses related to his problem/topic of research. Not only that, the facts elicited by the historians from varied sources do not speak by themselves, the historian has to give them flesh and blood, the garb and couch them, providing them the apparatus for speech where they address themselves. All facts about anything may not be known at a time – there may be gaps and missing links which the historian connects by his imagination.

A historian should adopt an objective approach to the facts and must take up an analytical view in order to get complete mastery over the facts and perfect control over the synthetic view of facts. He should be able to trace out the sequence of events by finding out the relations between events and events, and between events and environment. The circumstances and environment are very crucial factors to understand an event, without that, historical facts and data cannot be fruitfully applied. It is necessary to have an objective approach, both in discovering facts and interpreting them. But in order to be objective, the approach must be based on relevant, adequate and reliable data. A historian must be familiar with the general field of his topic and be clear with regards to his own objective.[11]

A historian should be skeptical about the view of other historians including himself, specially where in concluding the evidence the theory of probability has been applied and should be ready to change or modify his view in case he finds a new or more convincing evidence to the contrary. He should himself scan and screen through the primary source material himself to find out the shortfalls or inconsistencies if any. "The digging and delving once done, the next step is to verify and assemble the data; after which we are led to ask : what is the value of the "story" we recover from records? How far can we trust our sources? What is the effect of bias? The mechanism of causation? The merit of philosophic systems?"[12]

The facts *never* "speak for themselves". They must be selected, *marshalled,* linked together, and given a voice. If every researcher produces a different picture from the same sources, and if on large subjects rival interpretations continue to flourish, how can the reader of any history or biography escape confusion and ultimate skepticism? But at some time or other the query "what is truth?" will occur to any seeker after facts or will be put to any one who reports : "This is what happened".[13]

A historian must realize that "Scissors and Paste" method of writing history i.e. collecting the facts and putting them in connecting order, is obsolete. The facts must be ascertained by thoroughly probing into the various sources, put in logical order, assimilated, interpreted with honesty and self-awareness thereby taking a chance to dissent and judge for himself. The researcher must time and again *imagine* the kind of source he would like to have before he can find it. This may help him some time to unearth a new source which may prove vital to resolve the problem at hand.[14] Apart from the library research the researcher must prepare himself for field investigations and laboratory experiments depending upon the topic and the needs of the study.

Nature of History

"The definitive historical work on any topic has not been written and never will be". History as a dialogue. Each age must reinterpret its own past. With advances in technique and with advances in self-awareness, history is constant re-writing and reinterpretation and it is also a cumulative development. As a dialogue between present and past, history should also be a dialogue between the historian and his reader. Correctly used, the critical apparatus of bibliography and reference is intended, not as a showmanship of pedantry, but as an aid to the reader in playing his part in the dialogue.[15]

The past, which a historian studies is not a dead past, but a living past. The reconstruction of the past is done on the basis of empirical evidence which does not consist in a mere recital of facts. The process governs the selection and interpretation of facts which makes them historical facts. The facts never come in pure form; they are always refracted through the mind of the historian. History cannot be written unless the historians can achieve some kind of contact with the mind of those about whom he is writing. History means interpretation and Carr does not mind calling it "a hard core of interpretation surrounded by a pulp of disputable facts."[16] There is no "objective" historical truth – we have an infinity of meanings, none more right than any other; however which should not mean that facts of history are in principle not amenable to objective interpretation. The historian is engaged on a continuous process of moulding his facts to his interpretation and his interpretation to his facts.[17]

We may also notice: "The affairs of men consists of a complication of circumstances, so intimately interwoven as to be hardly separable from each other . Each owes its birth to some preceding circumstance and each in turn becomes the prolific parent of others: each, during its existence, has its irreparable attributes and its kindred facts, materially affecting its character, and essential to be known in order to a right understanding of its nature."[18]

We would like to quote an episode from E.H. Carr to illustrate this point: Jones, returning from a party is over-drunk and is driving a car whose brakes have turned to be defective, and at a blind corner knocks down and kills Robinson who was crossing the road to buy cigarettes at the shop on the corner. After the mess had been cleared up, the postmortem of the event was being discussed for enquiry at the local police headquarters with the following queries :

1. Was it due to the driver's semi-intoxicated condition – in which case there might be crucial prosecution?
2. Was it due to the defective brakes – in which case something might be said to the garage which overhauled the car only the week before? Or
3. Was it due to the blind corner – in which case the road authorities might be invited to give the matter their attention?

In the meanwhile, two gentleman enter the scene who start telling that if Robinson had not happened to exhaust his stock of cigarettes that evening, he would not have been crossing the road and would not have been killed; that Robinson's desire for cigarettes was, therefore, the cause of his death; and that any enquiry which neglects this cause will be waste of time, and any conclusions drawn from it meaningless and futile. After the two gentlemen were sent out, it was pointed out that of course, Robinson was killed because he was a cigarette-smoker, it is true and logical but it is a remorseless logic. At the same time, it makes more sense if we suppose that the curbing of alcoholic indulgence in drivers, or a strict control over the condition of brakes, or an improvement in the siting of roads, might serve the end of reducing the number of traffic fatalities. But it made no sense at all to suppose that the number of traffic fatalities could be reduced by preventing people from smoking cigarettes – concludes Carr that our faculty of reason could be used to draw out positive and constructive explanations.[19]

We may take another example of civil and criminal cases brought for adjudication before the courts. After reviewing the evidence and hearing arguments on both sides:

1. A lower court pronounces severe punishment while a higher court adjudicates acquittal or even *vice-versa.*
2. The Supreme Court may pronounce punishment for some participants in the crime and acquittal or less punishment for others due to lack of sufficient evidence or their less involvement in the crime committed.
3. Even some participants in the crime who were earlier acquitted in the case may be roped in due to availability of concrete evidence with the passage of time in the final judgement and given punishment.
4. Sometimes a new evidence may add a new dimension to the case or even the court may be moved to look into the matter afresh as often happens in a Hindi movie where, when the alleged culprit is being hanged to death or life imprisonment is being pronounced for his confession, the intruder appears on the scene with confession of murder producing the evidence and changes the whole scenario.

All this happens in human affairs with the same material evidence at disposal as the judgements are different in the courts of law in many cases or with the new facts coming to light, the judgements are variant.

We are tempted to narrate a folk-tale to illustrate our point: A person was being hanged to death as he was found guilty of committing a murder. As per custom he was asked to express a last wish which if possible could be fulfilled. At this, the alleged culprit asked for a cigarette. After lighting it and having a puff he laughed with full peels of laughter looking towards the sky. When enquired, he came out stating that he was looking at the Almighty, the final deliverer of justice, whose ways are strange as he has not committed this murder but a few years earlier he did commit such a crime for which he was not even suspected, but now his turn has come to meet the punishment, which had been delayed mysteriously by God.

The above episode indicates that sometimes even the people are punished without committing a crime in a particular case; they may be even falsely implicated. The court of law is bound to deliver a judgement on the alleged culprit once the charges are framed and proved on evidence presented as the proverbial saying goes: " we have seen truthful people being hanged" *(sacche phansi chadhade dekhe).*

We find historians giving different interpretations on important events. We have earlier cited the example of the revolution of 1857 in Indian history. The French Revolution has been differently interpreted by Carlyle who has shown more knowledge about the understanding of man than mere knowledge of facts by applying, 'psychology of the mob' and his 'portraits of individual characters'. While Lefebvre as a historian of French Revolution applies a quasi-psychological approach to history and made an indepth study of the role of the French peasantry during the Revolution and as a Marxian accepted the existence of the class-struggle.[20] A. Goodwin, writing a brief compressed history of the French Revolution, recorded only the largest changes in the groups involved. He pointed out to the growing seriousness of the class conflict and the occurrence of the sectional movements while George Rude, writing a longer history of the crowd in the French Revolution, provided much more details of the riots in Paris describing precisely when and where they occurred, and which sub-groups were involved.[21]

It is the nature of history that the authors focus their writings on different aspects and draw their own conclusions, thus giving different interpretations and even evolve or follow different methodologies. In case the different conclusions enlarge the canvas of history by giving different colours and complexions to it; it creates a baffling complexity and confusion for a lay reader or for a student who is interested in precisely knowing one true version of the event.

Scientific Method

The first beginnings of the evolution of some thing like a scientific method may be found, approximately at the turn of the sixth and fifth centuries B.C. in ancient Greece – conjectures Popper. What happened there? What is new in this evolution? How do the ideas compare with the traditional myths, which came from the East and which he thinks, provided many of the decisive suggestions for the new ideas?

What matters is the new attitude towards the myths which Popper calls as the 'critical attitude'. In the place of a dogmatic handling of a doctrine (in which the whole interest lies in the preservation of an authentic tradition), we find a critical discussion of the doctrine. Some people begin to ask questions about it, they doubt the trustworthiness of the doctrine: its truth......In the place of traditional theory – in place of the myth – we find the tradition of criticizing theories (which at first themselves are hardly more than myths). It is only in the course of this critical discussion that observation is called in as a witness.[22]

In order to understand the "Scientific Method" we need to know how science has developed. We find no better choice than Popper who explains as follows. The task of science is partly theoretical-explanation – and partly practical – prediction and technical application.... In the course of the historical development of Science, many different methods and kinds of explanation have been regarded as acceptable ; but they all have one aspect in common: the various methods of explanation all consist of a *Logical deduction;* a deduction whose conclusion is the *explicandum* – a statement of the thing to be explained–and whose premisses consist of the *explicans* (a statement of explaining laws and conditions).

The main changes that have occurred in the course of history of science consist in the silent abandonment of certain implicit demands regarding the character of the *explicans* (that it can be intuitively grasped, that it is to be self-evident, etc.) demands that turn out not to be reconsilable with certain other demands whose crucial significance becomes more and more obvious as the time goes on; in particular the demand for the independent testability of the *explicans* (which forms the premisses and thus the very heart of the explanation). Thus an explanation is always the deduction of the *explicandum* from certain premisses, to be called *explicans*. Popper cites an example of a rat dying soon of eating 'rat poison' and states: "But suppose for a moment that we are living in a world in which anybody (and also any rat) who eats a lot of that chemical called 'rat poison' will feel especially well and happy for a week to come and more lively than even before. If a universal law like this were valid, could the statement: 'This rat has eaten rat poison' still be acceptable as the explanation of death? Obviously not. Thus we have reached the important result, often overlooked, that any explanation that utilizes the singular initial conditions alone would be incomplete, and that at least *one universal law* is needed besides, even though this law is, in some cases, so well known that it is omitted as if it were redundant. To sum up this point we have found that an explanation is a deduction of the following kind:

U (Universal Law) ————> premisses
I (Special initial conditions) ———> constituting the *Explicans*
E (Explicandum) ————> conclusion

We should have, to submit the universal law to test cases which are independent of our *explicandum.* For example the death of a rat by reference to rat poison,–is it a satisfactory explanation? We do not know: the tests may show that whatever the rat may have died of, it was not rat poison. If some friend should be skeptical of our explanation and ask 'how do you know that this rat ate poison?' It will obviously not be sufficient to answer. 'How can you doubt it, seeing that it is dead?' If on the other hand, we are able to reply: 'Analyse the contents of its stomach and you will find a lot of poison', and if this prediction (which is new–that is not entailed by the *Explicandum* alone) proves true, we shall at least consider our explanation a fairly good hypothesis. But Popper wants to add something. For our skeptical friend may also question the truth of the universal law. He may say, for instance, 'granted this rat has eaten a certain chemical; but why should it have died of it?' Again we must not answer 'But don't you see it is dead?' That just shows you, how dangerous it is to eat this chemical'. For this again would make our explanation circular and unsatisfactory. In order to make it satisfactory we should have to submit the universal law to test cases which are independent of our *explicandum.*[23]

The state of affairs described by the singular *initial conditions* can be called the "cause" and the one described by the *explicandum* the "effect". But these terms acquire a meaning only relative to a theory or a universal law. It is the theory or the law which constitutes the logical link between cause and effect.[24]

Popper further points out "There is no road, royal or otherwise, which leads of necessity from a 'given' set of specific facts to any universal law. What we call 'laws' are hypotheses or conjectures which always form a part of some larger system of theories (in fact, a whole horizon of explanations) and which, therefore, can never be tested in isolation. The progress of science consists in trials, in elimination of errors, and in further trials guided by the experience acquired in the course of previous trials and errors.[25]

> "No particular theory may even be regarded as absolutely certain: every theory may become problematical, no matter how well corroborated it may seem now. No scientific theory is sacrosanct or beyond criticism."[26]

Even Popper admits his earlier definition of 'verisimilitude' to be faulty and improves it by stating "it can be solved by purely logical means but solely by a relativization to relevant problems or even by bringing in a historical problem stituation".[27] We regard the truth of a sentence as its 'Correspondence with reality'.[28]

It is through the falsifications of our suppositions that we actually get in touch with 'reality'. It is the discovery and elimination of our errors which alone constitute that 'positive' experience which we gain form reality. Popper is very brilliant in his observation when he deals with the oft-quoted enigma of the egg or the hen: The question 'What comes first, the hypothesis (H) or the observation (O)? reminds one, of course, of that other famous question: 'What came first, the hen (H) or the egg (O) ??' Both questions are soluble. The bucket theory asserts that (just as a primitive form of an egg (O), a unicellular organism, precedes the hen (H)): observation always precedes every hypothesis (H); for the bucket theory regards the latter (H) as arising from observations by generalization, or association, or classification. By contrast, we can now say that the hypothesis (or expectation or theory or whatever we may call it) precedes the observation, even though an observation that refutes a certain hypothesis may stimulate a new (and therefore a temporarily later) hypothesis.[29]

All this applies, more especially, to the formation of scientific hypotheses. For we learn only from our hypotheses what kind of observations we ought to make: whereto we ought to take an interest. "Thus it is the hypothesis which becomes our guide, and which leads us to new observational results.[30]

To reinforce his point further Popper calls this theory as stated above as the 'Searchlight theory' which he contrasts with the 'Bucket theory'. The 'Bucket theory' is a view held by Bacon and in a more radical form by Kant which is based on the theory that our knowledge, our experience consists either of accumulated perceptions ('naive empiricism' as remarked by Popper) or else of assimilated, sorted, and classified perceptions, according to which, our mind resembles a container – a kind of bucket – in which perceptions and knowledge accumulate.[31]

According to 'Searchlight theory' advocated by Popper, observations are secondary to hypotheses. Observations play, however, an important role as *tests* which a hypothesis must undergo in the course of our (critical) examination of it. If the hypothesis does not pass the examination; if it is falsified by our observations, then we have to look around for new hypothesis. In this case, the new hypothesis will come after those observations which led to the falsification or rejection of the old hypothesis. Yet what made the observations interesting and relevant, and what altogether gave rise to our understanding them in the first instance, was the earlier, the old (and now rejected) hypothesis.

In this way, science appears clearly as a straight forward continuation of the pre-scientific repair-work on our horizons of expectations. Science never starts from a scratch; it can never be described as free from assumptions, for at every instant it presupposes a horizon of expectations – yesterday's horizon of expectations, as it were. Today's science is built upon yesterday's science (and so it is the result of yesterday's searchlight) and yesterday's science, in turn, is based on the science of the day before. And the oldest scientific theories are built on pre-scientific myths, and these, in their turn, on still older expectations.[32]

We have already discussed how history differs from the natural and exact sciences. According to some scholars, Einstein's theory of relativity has not only dethroned the Newtonian absolutes but has revolutionized the thinking of man, where scientists also deal in probabilities which the social scientists are doing following them. Since there are no absolutes in the natural sciences, when the historian fails to establish conclusive proofs for his version of past events he may not necessarily be exposing himself as thoroughly unscientific. The historian can only show from his sources that it was likely, or most probable, that something happened in the way he says it did. However, most of the scholars are of the view that the critical methods which we use in the acquisition of historical information are as scientific as those of laboratory or the field expedition and that it is not in method that social science differs from physical science but in the nature of phenomena they study.[33]

Science has been defined as ' systematised, organised, formulated knowledge', and history, the original meaning of which is investigation, is therefore a science if it is pursued with the sole purpose of ascertaining the truth, if all relevant facts are diligently searched for, if presuppositions and prejudices are eliminated, if the constants and the variables are noted and plotted with the same care that is the rule in the natural sciences.[34]

The locus of historical reality is not in the mind of historian but in the past events in which the historian had no say or hand; the historian only tries to build an account of the past and 'creates' history only up to that point. The objective of historical research is to uncover the shape of past and it involves searching out the 'sources', cxamining there dependability and making them yield faithful informations.[35] Unlike the fiction writer who works on "What could have happened?" the historian is concerned with "What did happen?"

The acceptability of the interpretation of the historical data also depends upon its determinate factual basis: It should not be either arbitrary or imaginative but based on reason, correspondence and coherence–correspondence and coherence with the body of knowledge already existing in the field. Cross-checking and verification of data had always been the most important aspect of the methodology of history since the time of Herodotus and Thucydides.[36]

Scientific method is a collective term denoting the various processes by the aid of which the sciences are build up. In a wide sense, any method of investigation by which, scientific or other impartial or systematic knowledge is acquired is called a scientific method.[37] Observation, hypothesis and verification are three procedural components in a scientific approach. There is no monism in scientific method. Different stages of enquiry may have different scientific methods, and the method which is scientific for one stage may not be so for another. It aims at discovering the actual facts and establishing their inter-connection. After thorough weighing of the evidence, it may formulate some general propositions. It is not the facts themselves which make science but the method by which they are dealt with. Scientific method, being highly elastic can be applied to all domains of human activity where the discovery of the truth is the objective.[38]

More specifically, scientific method can be defined as consisting of four major parts:

1. Identification of the problem;
2. Formulation of a hypothesis which is deemed as a tentative conclusion;
3. Systematically collecting, classifying, and analysing data; and
4. Either acceptance or rejection of the hypothesis.

There are scholars who state that there is no such thing as the scientific method. The methods of science vary from one field of enquiry to another, may be peculiar to the discipline of science in which they are used. However, it is possible to find a pattern common to virtually all scientific research, which we may call Scientific technique, which also consists of four elements or steps:

1. The assembly of facts or existing information;

2. The formation of a hypothesis or hypotheses; i.e. the formation of a system of general propositions to explain the behaviour of the facts;
3. The prediction, which is an explanation obtained by deducing from the hypothesis specific conclusions not already known from the mere collection of facts; and
4. The testing or the prediction by reference again to observed facts.[39]

The learning of the facts of a particular branch of science without knowing how to derive them or other presently unknown facts is really not possessing a scientific attitude of mind which is the thresher of facts and connector of facts – nothing is more valuable than the mastering of sound principles of methodology.[40]

Facts are not only to be known but also to be ascertained. There is an ardent need to discriminate between what is true and what is false, what is probable and what is doubtful or impossible, which rests on a combination of knowledge, skepticism, faith, common sense, and intelligent guessing.[41] When there are several speculations over any happening, "the historian must try to reach a decision and make it rationally convincing, not only to himself, but to others. The steps by which he performs this task constitute verification."[42] Verification is done on a multitude of points – from getting an author's first name correct to proving that a document is both genuine and authentic. In other words it is not a forged one and truthfully reports on its ostensible subject "Verification is conducted on many planes, and its technique is not fixed. It relies on attention to detail, on commonsense reasoning, on a developed 'feel' for history and chronology, on familiarity with human behaviour, and on ever enlarging stores of information."[43] In case it is necessary to test the accuracy of a story or a legend, the first step is to trace the tale to its origin.[44]

An autobiography may be deemed both as a primary source and a secondary source as well– primary source for the account of the author's experiences and thoughts and a secondary history of the times through which the writer has lived. Usually composed long after the events described, an autobiography will usually have to be treated with even greater circumspection than the more straight forward primary document.[45] In autobiographies, one must be prepared to find errors in dates and names without necessarily inferring that the account is false.[46]

Similarly *Memoirs* may give a "short-circuiting" picture of an event unless written with the aid of a diary or a full correspondence file.[47]

Similarly, in case of contemporary history, the history of events through which the historian has himself lived, may have some of the eye-witness quality of a primary record. This again may be of two kinds, one written by a reputed historian about the period in a detached manner as far as possible and the other by actual participants in the events narrated.[48]

Marwick does not seem to give credence to the imaginative literature left by an age or generation. At the most, a historian can draw from it an insight into the *mores* and *folkways* of the period; he can familiarise himself with the literature of a particular period or topic, in the end make no direct reference to, or quote from any specific novel or poem.[49] He can gain himself his understanding of his period which may help him to satisfy his quest from his other sources, but it may not have given him one single piece of concrete information.[50]

In case of a letter being traced out related to an event, it should be received with caution and tested bit by bit – though the possibility of forgery, tampering and substitution cannot be ruled out. Once it has stood the test of scrutiny, its probative value is fully as great as the testimony of witness and often greater. The 'circumstantial evidence' of the law courts is a familiar example of this type of mute testimony.[51]

Authenticity of Sources of History

Sources of history are the traces left by human thought and needs in the past. The study of reliability of information involves both external and internal criticism of a source and that external criticism be identified with the study of authenticity of sources and internal criticism, with the study of the reliability of information.[52]

External Criticism

External criticism involves the authorship, the date and the place of the origin of the source which may include its comparison with other sources. For this the historian may ask a number of questions:

1. Is the document authentic, is it what it purports to be?
2. How did the document come into existence in the first place?
3. Who exactly was the author, that is, apart from his name, what role in society did he play, what sort of person was he?
4. What was his purpose of writing it?

Internal Criticism

Internal criticism deals with the contents of the work, their probability and the author's veracity. First thing to do is to analyse the contents and then try to understand under what conditions it was produced , so as to know the real and correct meaning of author's statements.

Actually both the external and internal criticisms go together. We can know the truth of author's statements by our knowledge about the author, his predicament, constraints and compulsions if any.[53]

We have to compare and contrast the information about the Mauryan times in the *Arthasastra* of Kautilya with that of Megasthenes's *Indica.* Similarly, about the description of Akbar's reign we may compare and contrast the account of Abul Fazal's with that of Badauoni's.

We should also compare and contrast the new edition of a work with the first edition and may notice some changes and modifications. Webster has quoted the example of Lala Lajpat Rai's *The Arya Samaj,* originally published in 1915 appraising of many changes not only in the recasting of chapters but also the modification in the statements of the original author in the revised and expanded edition by Sri Ram Sharma published in 1967.[54] After verifications of our sources, we take down facts from them and verify them from the factual statements.

Facts and the Relevancy of Facts

Fact: The Concise Oxford Dictionary defines the fact as a "thing certainly known to have occurred or be true."[55]

For further elaboration on the point we are tempted to quote from a law-book. According to the *Law of Evidence* 'The Indian Evidence Act' :

"Fact" means and includes:

(1) Any thing, state of things, or relation of things capable of being perceived by the senses; and

(2) Any mental condition of which any person is conscious. One fact is said to be relevant to another when the one is concerned with the other in any of the ways relating to the relevancy of facts.

The word 'relevant' is used with two distinct meanings:

(a) as admissible,

(b) as connected.

"Of all rules of evidence, the most universal and the most obvious is this,–that the evidence adduced should be alike directed and confined to the matters which are in dispute, or which form the subject of investigation".

'Facts in issue' means the matters which are in dispute or which form the subject of decision and whether the evidence offered is relevant *to any of them.*

While a "Document" means any matter expressed or described upon any substance by means of letters, figures or marks, or by more than one of these means, intended to be used, or which may be used, for the purpose of recording that matter.

"Evidence" means and includes

1. All statements which the court presents or requires to be made before it by witness, in relation to matters of fact under enquiry: such statements are called oral evidence;
2. All documents produced for the inspection of the court:

such documents are called documentary evidence.

(i) "Proved": A fact is said to be proved when, after considering the matters before it, the court either believes it to exist, or considers its existence so probable that a prudent man ought, under the circumstances of the particular case, to act upon the supposition that it exists.

(ii) "Disproved": A fact is said to be disproved when, after considering the matters before it, the court either believes that it does not exist or considers its non-existence so probable that a prudent man ought, under the circumstances of the particular case, to act upon the supposition that it does not exist.

(iii) "Not Proved": A fact is said not to be proved when it is neither proved nor disproved. Whenever, it is provided by this Act that the court may presume a fact, it may either regard such fact as 'proved, unless and until it is disproved, or may call for proof of it:

Whenever, it is directed by this Act that the court shall presume a fact, it shall regard such fact as proved, unless and until it is disproved.

"Conclusive Proof": when one fact is declared by this Act to be conclusive proof of another, the court shall, on proof of the one fact, regard the other as proved, and shall not allow evidence to be given for the purpose of disproving it.[56]

Of the Relevancy of Facts

Evidence may be given of facts in issue and relevant facts. Facts which, though not in issue, are so connected with a fact in issue as to form part of the same transaction, are relevant, whether they occurred at the same time and place or at different times and places.

Facts which are the occasion, cause or effect, immediate or otherwise, of relevant facts or facts in issue, or which constitute the state of things under which they happened, or which afforded an opportunity for their occurrence or transaction, are relevant.

Any fact is relevant which shows or constitutes a motive or preparation for any fact in issue or relevant fact.

Facts necessary to explain or introduce a fact in issue or relevant fact, or which support or rebut an inference suggested by a fact in issue or relevant fact, or which establish the identity of any thing or person whose identity is relevant, or fix the time or place at which any fact in issue or relevant fact happened or which show the relation of parties by whom any such fact was transacted, are relevant in so far as they are necessary for that purpose.

When there is a reasonable ground to believe that two or more persons have conspired together to commit an offence or an actionable wrong, any thing said, done or written by any one of such persons in reference to their common intention, after the time when such intention was first entertained by any one of them, is *a relevant fact* as against each of the persons believed, to be so conspiring, as well for the purpose of proving the existence of the conspiracy as for the purpose of showing that such person was a party to it.

Facts not otherwise relevant are relevant:

1. If they are inconsistent with any fact in issue or relevant fact:
2. If by themselves or in connection with other facts they make the existence or non-existence of any fact in issue or relevant fact highly probable or improbable.

In suits in which damages are claimed, any fact which will

enable the court to determine the amount of damages which ought to be awarded, is relevant.

When the question is as to the existence of any right or custom, the following facts are relevant:

(a) any transaction by which the right or custom in question was created, claimed, modified, recognized, asserted or denied, or which was inconsistent with its existence; and

(b) particular instances in which the right or custom was claimed, rccognized or exercised, or in which its exercise was disputed, asserted or departed from Facts showing the existence of any state of mind, such as intention, knowledge, good faith, negligence, rashness, ill-will or good-will towards any particular person, or showing the existence of any state of body or bodily feeling, *are relevant,* when the existence of any such state of mind or body or bodily feeling is an issue or relevant.

(1) A fact relevant as showing the existence of a relevant state of mind must show that the state of mind exists, not generally, but in reference to the particular matter in question.

(2) But where, upon the trial of a person accused of an offence, the previous commission by the accused of an offence is relevant within the meaning of this section, the previous conviction of such person also will be a relevant fact.

When there is a question whether an act was accidental or intentional, or done with a particular knowledge or intention, the fact that such act formed part of a series of similar occurrences, in each of which the person doing the act was concerned, is relevant. When there is a question whether a particular act was done, the existence of any course of business, according to which it naturally would have been, is a relevant fact.[57]

The elaboration as stated above shows that not only the facts need to be known but collateral facts also need to be known for ascertaining them.

Factual Statements

Popper applies the principle of empiricism in the analysis of factual statements. He states that only 'experience' can help us to make up our minds about the truth or falsity of factual statements. A statement is true if and only if it corresponds to the facts.[58] Further he states: "All our theories are man-made and that we try to impose them upon the world of nature. The question whether our man-made theories are true or not depend upon the real facts; real facts which are, with very few exceptions, emphatically not man-made. Our man-made theories may clash with these real facts, and so, in our search for truth, we may have to adjust our theories or to give them up. Tarski's theory allows us to define truth as corresponding to the facts, but we can use it also to *define reality* as that to which true statements correspond. For example, we may distinguish *real facts,* that is (alleged) facts that are real, from (alleged) facts that are not real (that is from non-facts) or to put it more explicately, we can say that an alleged fact is not a real fact or it is not a fact at all. And just as Tarski allows us to replace the term 'truth' by 'the set of true statements (or sentences)', so we can replace the term 'reality' by 'the set of real facts'.[59]

At one place Popper ridicules the labouring, the difference between science and the humanities. The method of problem-solving, the method of conjecture and refutation is practised by both. It is practised in reconstructing a damaged text as well as in constructing the theory of radioactivity. Further, he denounces the histories trying to copy the method of natural science, that is collecting observations and then 'drawing conclusions' from them–the historians who believe that they can collect documentary evidence which, corresponding to the observations of material science, forms the 'empirical basis' for their conclusions.

This alleged method is one that can never be put into effect: you can neither collect observations nor documentary evidence *if you do not first have a problem* (A ticket collector collects documents, but he rarely collects historical evidence). If we do not dare to tackle problems which are so difficult that error is almost unavoidable, then there will be no growth of knowledge. In fact, it is from our boldest theories, including those which are erroneous, that we learn most. Nobody is exempt from making mistakes, the great thing is to learn from them.[60]

The stormy development of Physics since the turn of the century has taught us better, and we have now come to see that it is the task of the scientist to subject his theory to ever new tests and that no theory must be pronounced final. Testing proceeds by taking the theory to be tested and combining it with all possible initial conditions as well as with other theories, and then comparing the resulting predictions with reality. If this leads to disappointed expectations, to refutations then we have to rebuild our theory...... It is the discovery and examination of our errors which alone constitute that 'positive' experience which we gain from reality.[61]

What we attempt in science is to describe and (so far as possible) explain reality.[62] Popper talks of approximation to the truth or of a nearness to truth or 'verisimilitude' which combines two notions : (a) the notion of truth, and (b) the notion of the (logical) content of a statement; that is, the class of all statements logically entailed by it. He calls it by one word "truthfulness". He compares the Newtonian and Einsteinian theories of gravitation and calls Einstein's theory potentially or virtually the better theory being the theory with greater content i.e., it has the greater explanatory power. The theory with the greater content will also be one with the greater verisimilitude *unless its falsity content is also greater.* This assertion forms the logical basis of method of science–the method of bold conjectures and of attempted definitions. A theory,–the bolder–the greater its content. It is also the riskier. It is more probable to start with that it will be false. We try to find its weak points to refute it. If we fail to refute it or if the refutations we find are at the same time also refutations of the weaker theory which was its predecessor, then we have reason to suspect, or to conjecture that the stronger theory has no greater falsity content than its weaker predecessor, and, therefore, that it has the greater degree of verisimilitude. The growth of all knowledge consists in the modification of previous knowledge–either its alteration or its large scale rejection. The method of science is the method of bold conjectures and ingenious and severe attempts to refute them.[63]

In science it is *observation* rather than perception which plays the decisive part. But observation is a process in which we play an intensively active part. An observation is a perception, but one which is planned and prepared. An observation is always preceded by a particular interest, a question, or a problem–in short, by something theoretical (by which Popper means 'speculative') After all, we can put every question or conjecture to which we add: "Is this so? Yes or no?" Thus we can assert that every observation is preceded by a problem, a hypothesis (or whatever we may call it); at any rate by something that interests us, by something theoretical or speculative. This is why observations are always selective, and why they presuppose something like a principle of selection.[64]

Popper points out the difference between the tasks of a theoretical and of a historical explanation. The theoretician is interested in finding and testing universal laws. In the course of testing them he uses other laws, of the most diverse kinds (many of them quite unconsciously) as well as diverse specific initial conditions. The historian on the other hand is interested in finding descriptions of states of affairs in certain finite, specific spatio-temporal regions –that is to say what he calls specific initial conditions – and in testing or checking their adequacy or accuracy. In this kind of testing he uses, in addition to other specific initial conditions universal laws of all kinds–usually rather obvious ones – which belong to the horizon of expectations, though as a rule, he is not conscious that he uses them. In this he resembles the theoretician. Their difference, however, is very marked: it lies in the difference between their various interests, or problems: in the difference what each regards as problematic.[65]

Popper advocates that we should dare to put forward bold hypotheses that open up, if possible, new domains of observations rather than those careful generalizations from 'given' observations which have remained (ever since Bacon) the idols of all naïve empiricists. He further exhorts that our theories should be testable. Yet there are degrees of testability. Some theories are better testable than others….. The testability of a theory grows with its degree of universality as with its degree of definiteness or precision. Popper is of the view that it is through the falsification of our suppositions that we actually get in touch with 'reality'.[66]

Interpretation in History

The problem of understanding in history, according to Popper, is problem about a problem, a higher level problem– a case of objective historical understanding.

Popper states that the main aim of all historical understanding is the hypothetical reconstruction of a historical problem situation in which this problem arose? For which he pleads for application of situational logic or situational analysis. Out of the two terms, he prefers to make use of situational analysis by which he means a certain kind of tentative or conjectural explanation of some human action which appeals to the situation in which the agent finds himself. It may be a historical explanation: we may perhaps wish to explain how and why a certain structure of ideas was created? We can try, conjecturally, to give an idealized, reconstruction of the problem situation in which the agent found himself and to that extent made the action 'understandable' (or rationally 'understandable'), that is to say, adequate to his situation as he saw it. Popper names this method of situational analysis as an application of the rationality principle.

We must distinguish between the situation as the agent saw it and the situation as it was (both, of course, conjectured). This may be used as an explanatory theory of human action, which consists of a conjectural reconstruction of the problem and its background. It can be testable. It may even be applied to works of art: we may conjecture what the artist's problem was, and we may be able to support this conjecture by independent evidence, and this analysis, may help us to understand the work.[67]

Popper quotes from Collingwood's *Idea of History*[68] in this connection Collingwood calls for re-enactment of the experience of the emperor in historian's mind in case he is writing on an emperor's action and only in doing so he makes contribution to historical knowledge as distinct from merely philosophical knowledge –he must envisage the situation as that emperor envisaged it.[69] Popper comments that Collingwood's stress upon situation is diametrically opposed to his (Popper's) idea of problem situation as Popper regards as essential not the re-enactment but the situational analysis. The historian, being on a level different from the emperor's reasoning does not re-enact it, but tries to produce an idealized and reasoned reconstruction of it, omitting inessential elements and perhaps augmenting it. There the historian's central meta problem is: what were the decisive elements in the emperor's problem situation? To the extent to which the historian succeeds in solving the meta-problem, he understands the historical situation. Thus historian has not to re-enact past experiences, but to marshal objective arguments for and against his conjectural situational analysis. This method may be very successful even in those cases in which an attempt at the re-enactment necessarily fails–for there may be acts beyond the capacity of a historian for action and therefore for re-enactment. Even if in some cases, it is possible it may be superfluous. The historian's task is, therefore, so to reconstruct the problem situation as it appeared to the agent, that the actions of the agent become adequate to the situation.[70] This is very similar to Collingwood's method, but it eliminates from the theory of understanding and from the historical method precisely the subjective or second-world element which for Collingwood and most other theorists of understanding (hermeneuticists) is its silent point. Our conjectural reconstruction of the situation may be a real historical discovery. It may explain an aspect of history so far unexplained, and it may be corroborated by new evidence, for example by the fact that it may improve our understanding of some previously overlooked or unexplained allusions.[71]

The element of interpretation enters into every fact of history. The facts speak only when the historian gives them a floor and places them in some order or context[72]. According to E.H. Carr, a historian needs 'imaginative understanding' for the minds of the people with whom he is dealing, for the thought behind their acts.[73]

It is equally important to study the historian or the author of a particular major work which is our source of information for the period or the subject under investigation. We should try to understand his motive for the work before we can utilise the material information provided by it. For example Engel's *Conditions of the English Working Class* (1845) where Engels has tried to paint as black picture as possible of working-class conditions and of the wickedness of their capitalistic exploiters. We cannot take his descriptive matter entirely at face value, though his eye-witness accounts stand as primary sources; much of the book, however, is taken from newspaper accounts and from government papers ; the historian must himself go directly to the sources from which Engels quotes, and in some cases, misquotes. The work is a most important primary source for the study of socialist thought, though Engels essentially wrote his book with a specific, definite purpose–the exposure of the evils of capitalism.[74]

Fact and Generalization

Historian is equally concerned both with the unique and the general. History thrives on generalizations–that is what distinguishes the historian from the collector of historical facts.[75] Generalization has been explained in the dictionary as : (Forming of) general notion or proposition obtained by induction with a caution about hasty generalization the one based on too few instances[76]. Induction has been defined as inferring of general law from particular instances (*cf.* deduction)[77] while deduction has been explained as inference from general to particular (*cf.* induction).[78]

In deduction we deduce generalization from universal to particular thus the deductive method gives us conclusions which are certain. But in induction we arrive at universal generalizations from particular facts, hence the conclusion of the inductive method are only probable and not always certain[79]. To describe both the departments of logic, deduction and induction briefly, proof from principles and proof from facts.[80] Deduction and induction are complementary rather than competitive, like the right and left foot are needed for walking. In sciences, the two methods are used side by side and the combination of the two methods is known as Deductive-Inductive method or logical positivism. This method is extensively used in scientific investigation.

Ghosh[81] describes this method in the following four main stages:

1. Feeling the problem.
2. Formulation of hypothesis.
3. Deductive development of hypothesis.
4. Verification of hypothesis.

Topolski[82] classifies generalizations into the following seven categories :

(i) Generalizations varying as to the degree of generality – according to the scope of generalised knowledge of specific facts;

(ii) Factographic generalizations (which point to established facts);

(iii) Causal generalizations which formulate results of causal explanations;

(iv) Exception free generalizations;

(v) Reporting generalizations – they are simple conjunctions of statements about single established facts ;

(vi) Hypothetical generalizations; and

(vii) Statistical generalizations.

"Historians often sum up what they know about an historical subject in generalizations and classificatory statements". McCullagh remarks that "These summaries usually present a general view of the subject which the historian thinks interesting. Different historians frequently describe the same subject slightly differently, depending upon their interests and the concepts with which they are familiar. It is quite appropriate to call these summary general descriptions 'interpretations' of the subject, meaning that they are one of several equally justified accounts of the subject which could be given, which provides the reader with at least the historian's opinion of the opinion of the meaning of what was happening."[83]

Some philosophers of history while admitting the descriptions of particular events, suspect the picture of reality that generalizations and classificatory descriptions provide. McCullagh quotes from F.R. Ankersmit who states that historical concepts like Renaissance and the Fall of the Roman Empire, are defined differently by different historians and refutes his criticism about reality in strong terms. "Consequently, it is abusurd to say that they refer to facts in the world. Rather they represent historians' ideas about the past, not the past itself".[84] On Ankersmit's denial to detect common features among different states, revolutions and so on, to arrive at general concepts of these things presumably because each instance is so different that they lack sufficient common features.

McCullagh reacts strongly stating that the different instances of general terms are always unique in detail, but that does not stop us from classifying them e.g., chairs and dogs are again classified into kinds of chairs and breeds of dog, the fact that they differ so much does not prevent their being instances of chairs and dogs, because they all share the essential characteristics of chairs and dogs, and asserts that the same is true of general concepts used to characterize the past. Individual instances of them differ in detail, but all share the same common characteristics.[85] However, McCullagh agrees that some classificatory terms are quite vague and their vagueness can sometimes lead historians to dispute their applicability.[86] He quotes the use of the term 'Revolution' used by G.R.Elton in the functioning of the Government of England between 1532 and 1540 which raked up a big debate among the historians whether these changes could be characterized as revolutionary at all. It was not clear whether one could say that a revolution in government had occurred when constitutional and administrative principles had changed substantially. The critics of Elton's thesis argued that the changes under Cromwell were not revolutionary because they did not constitute a sudden change in the nature of English Government.[87]

In this context, we may quote the use of the term 'Feudalism' in Indian history, which almost every serious student of history is aware of and the debate it has raised among the historians which still remains inconclusive.

For explanation in history historian, is concerned both with the direct and indirect evidence which in Indian system or science of logic consists of four types of evidences:

(1) *Pratyaksha :* A thing which is seen by us like a *Amalaka* fruit in our hand. That is why in any event or happening, the eye-witness is very important.

(2) *Anumana :* Assumption or guess-work. Seeing something before our eyes we can assume some act already accomplished..., even not directly seen by us, with the help of our common knowledge.

(3) *Upamana:* Analogy : We can also know something by analogy.

(4) *Sabda:* Voice or sound: We also understand things by the voice or sound they make or create.

Apart from this we are equally concerned with the logical and illogical, or rational or irrational behaviour of man to understand human action where the same man is a changed man next moment, the same man behaving differently with different persons as well as in different situations, showing extreme reaction or excessive reaction to some action which is quite different and complex in comparison to the tools and techniques of a scientist in a laboratory.[88]

In India, we have an old tradition of *Shastrartha* (discussion) to decide or clinch the issues at hand by hearing both sides, weighing the arguments on either side and then concluding the decision on the basis of the weight of evidence on either side by our wisdom.

The same method is, in fact, followed in the civil and criminal proceedings in the courts of law, though some difference is practised for weighing the evidence in civil and criminal proceedings: "The rules of evidence are in general the same in civil and criminal proceedings, and bind alike crown and subject, prosecutor and accused, plaintiff and defendant. There are, however, some exceptions e.g., doctrine of estoppel applies to civil proceedings only. The provisions relating to confessions, character of persons appearing before court and incompetence of parties as witnesses are peculiar to criminal proceedings. But there is a strong and marked difference as to the *effect* of evidence in civil and criminal proceedings. In the former, a mere preponderance of probability, due regard to being had to the burden of proof, is a sufficient basis of decision; but in the latter, especially when the offence charged amounts to treason or felony, a much higher degree of assurance is required. The serious consequences of an erroneous condemnation, both to the accused and society, the immeasurably greater evils which flow from it than from an erroneous acquittal have induced the laws of every wise and civilised nation to lay down the principle, though often lost sight of in practice, that the persuasion of the guilt ought to amount to a moral certainty: such a moral certainty as convinces the minds of the tribunal, as reasonable men, beyond all reasonable doubt."[89] This shows the application of theory of relativity in human affairs. The punishment in a criminal case should not be pronounced on an alleged guilt until and unless the guilt is proved on the person concerned beyond doubt. Recent advances in DNA technology are helping the courts to resolve some complex causes of parentage of the children related to the sexual abuses and involvement of inheritance to property rights as well as the murder and rape cases. Recently in Everett (Washington), new DNA testing methods have led the police to arrest James Stephens Jr. who was first charged in the murder of his sister-in-law 23 years ago. Though Stephens was charged with first degree murder and first degree rape, but the charges were dismissed without prejudice meaning they could be refiled because of lack of evidence. Stephens though working for a shipping company, was kept under intermittent surveillance by police. The case was reopened two years ago, when advances in DNA allowed for very good results even when the evidence was in bad shape–the key DNA tests found a perfect match between a recent blood sample taken from Stephens and a semen stain on the shirt worn by Kuntz when she was killed. This major breakthrough came just a week ago which made the police to arrest Stephens and charge him for the rape and stabbing of Kuntz.[90]

Now-a-days it as being realised that a "multi-centric" or better call it " multi-method" approach is required to deal with certain topics in history or historical issues to reach the approximation to the truth. For example while writing on the *Freedom Movement in India,* it is deemed advisable to interview the living freedom fighters and record their evidence. For a work on *Economic History of India*, it is advisable to use the quantitative methods which may involve computer applications in historical research.[91] Similarly, when a topic on Art or Epigraphy or Numismatics where the specific evidence is based on the specified disciplines, we ought to refer to evidence from other related sources such as literature, ethnography[92] and archaeology even though largely relying on artefacts, inscriptional or numismatic data depending on the specified topic. Some degree of collaboration and corroboration of the data from other sources of the period or area of study is required to conclude the thesis. If we are working on a particular art form e.g. paintings of a particular period or region, depending on the topic, it is essential to interview the concerned living artists in the area of specialisation to arrive at the thorough understanding of the themes and perspectives related to the study rather than simply depending on the available data found or traced out in the contemporary written sources. Winding up the discussion on research methodology here we shall treat some related issues in the following chapters on *Causation in History and Objectivity in History.*

Notes

1. Herbert Butterfield, *The Whig Interpretation of History,* New York, 1931, Norton Imprint, 1965 p.132.
2. Jacques Barzun & Henry F. Graff, *The Modern Researcher,* New York, 1977 p.13.
3. Fritz Stern (ed.) *The Varieties of History,* London, 1956, Second edn. 1970 p. 364.
4. Irfan Habib, *Interpreting Indian History,* North-Eastern Hill University Publications Shillong, p. 1.
5. P.N. Chopra, *The Gazetteer of India*, Volume II, P.IL.
6. John C.B. Webster, *An Introduction to History,* Delhi, 1977, pp.61-63.
7. C. Behan McCullagh, *The Truth of History,* London, 1998, p. 5.
8. E.H. Carr, *What is History*? Penguin Books England, 1961, Reprinted 1965 p. 30.
9. T.R. Sharma, *The Concept of History,* Delhi, 1987, p. 1.
10. McCullagh, *The Truth of History*, pp. 169–171.
11. B.N. Ghosh, *Lecturers on Scientific Method,* New Delhi, 1986, pp. 29-30.
12. Barzun and Graff, *op. cit.,* Preface p. x.
13. *Ibid.*

14. *Ibid.*, pp. 47-50.
15. Arthur Marwick, *The Nature of History,* London, 1970, pp. 21-22.
16. E.H. Carr, *What is History?* pp. 22-23.
17. *Ibid.*, pp. 26-29.
18. Ratanlal Ranchhoddas & D.K. Thakore, *The Law of Evidence,* third edn. Bombay, : (The Bombay Law Reporter Office, 2A Charni Road), 1923 , p.17.
19. E.H. Carr, *op. cit.,* pp. 104-107.
20. Arthur Marwick, *op. cit.,* pp. 57, 63-67.
21. McCullagh, *op. cit.,* pp. 60-61.
22. *Ibid.*, pp. 346-347.
23. *Ibid.*, pp. 349-351.
24. *Ibid.*, p.352.
25. *Ibid.*, pp. 359 - 360.
26. *Ibid.*, p. 360.
27. *Ibid.*, p. 371.
28. *Ibid.*, p. 367.
29. *Ibid.*, p. 346.
30. *Ibid.*
31. *Ibid.*, pp. 341, 346.
32. *Ibid.* pp. 346-347.
33. Marwick, *op. cit.,* pp. 102-103.
34. *Ibid.*, Bernadotte Schmitt, *Fashion and Future of History* p. 23 as quoted by Marwick.
35. Sibesh Bhattacharya, "Historical Reality: Some Conceptual and Methodological Components" in Janak Pandey (ed.) *Social Reality,* New Delhi, 1988, pp. 95-96.
36. *Ibid.*, p. 100.
37. R.P. Misra, *Research Methodology,* New Delhi, 1988, p.6; Ghosh, *op. cit.,* p. 36.
38. Ghosh, *op. cit.,* p. 36.
39. R.P. Misra, *op. cit.,* pp. 7-8; Ghosh, *op. cit.,* p. 36.
40. Mishra, *op. cit.,* p. 7.
41. Barzun and Graff, *op. cit.,* p. 83.

42. *Ibid.*, p. 85.

43. *Ibid.*

44. *Ibid.*, p. 90.

45. Marwick, *op. cit.*, p. 134.

46. Barzun and Graff, *op. cit.*, p. 92.

47. *Ibid.*

48. Marwick, *op. cit.*, pp. 134-135.

49. *Ibid.*, pp. 138-139.

50. *Ibid.*, p. 139.

51. Barzun and Graff, *op. cit.*, pp. 92-93.

52. Jerzy Topolski, *Methodology of History,* Warsaw, 1973, USA, 1976, p. 432.

53. Marwick, *op. cit.*, pp. 136-137, Topolski, *op. cit.*, pp. 431-453, Barzun and Graff *op. cit.*, pp. 101-108.

54. C.B Webster, *An Introduction to History,* Delhi, 1977, pp. 72-74.

55. Fowler, H.W. and Fowler, F.B (eds.) *The Concise Oxford Dictionary,* OUP, 1959, p. 424, col. 2.

56. Ratanlal Ranchoddas and D.K. Thakore, *The Law of Evidence,* 3rd edn. Bombay, 1923, pp. 4-14.

57. *Ibid.*, pp. 15-50.

58. Karl R. Popper, *Objective Knowledge: An Evolutionary Approach,* Revised edition OUP, 1986 pp. 12, 46.

59. Popper, *op. cit.* pp. 328-329; Tarski, A, *Logic Semantics, Meta-Mathematics* tr. by J.H. Woodger, OUP, 1956, pp. 268-277.

60. Popper, *op. cit.*, pp. 185-186.

61. *Ibid.*, p. 360.

62. *Ibid.*, p. 40.

63. *Ibid.*, pp. 40, 47, 52-53, 71,81.

64. *Ibid.*, pp. 342-343.

65. *Ibid.*, p. 354.

66. *Ibid.*, pp. 354-356, 360.

67. *Ibid.*, pp. 170, 177-179.

68. R.G.Collingwood, *The Idea of History,* OUP, London, 1973, p. 283.

69. *Ibid.*, p. 187.

70. *Ibid.*, pp. 188-189.
71. *Ibid.*, p. 189.
72. E.H. Carr, *op. cit.*, pp. 11-13.
73. *Ibid.*, p. 24.
74. Marwick, *op. cit.*, p. 135.
75. E.H. Carr, *op. cit.*, pp. 64-65.
76. *The Concise Oxford Dictionary, op. cit.*, p. 499.
77. *Ibid.*, p. 609.
78. *Ibid.*, p. 311.
79. Ghosh, *op. cit.*, pp. 54-55.
80. Carveth Read, *Logic Deductive and Inductive,* London, Grant Richards, 1901 p. 4.
81. Ghosh, *op, cit.*, p. 57.
82. Topolski, *op. cit.*, p. 632.
83. McCullagh, *op. cit.*, p. 64.
84. *Ibid.*, p. 66.
85. *Ibid.*, pp. 66-67.
86. *Ibid.*, p. 68.
87. *Ibid.*
88. T.G. Ashplant; "Psycho-analysis in Historical Writing" in *History Workshop*, Issue 26, 1988, pp. 102.
89. Ratanlal Ranchhoddas and D.K. Thakore, *op. cit.*, pp. 10-11.
90. *The New Indian Express,* Hyderabad, June 19, 1999, p. 15.
91. Topolski, *op. cit.*, pp. 483-535.
92. D.D.Kosambi, *The Culture and Civilization of India in Historical Outline,* Delhi, 1972, Passim.

7

CAUSATION IN HISTORY

The historian or any curious reader will always like to know when told about some event or happening that why it so happened? Carr gives an example of setting out of boiling of milk in a saucepan which we may not even care to know and may probably attribute it to a propensity in milk to boil over.[1] But here also comes the question of time and space – boiling of milk over a gas – stove may take more time if the space changes from the plains to a hilly area. The same boiling of milk is seen with a different angle and accounted for a different cause by a literary person who cites it as a fine example of friendship between the water and milk–first the water burns itself and then milk responds that it will not stay in the saucepan and comes out–the example is quoted in a Sanskrit verse.

In the science of logic (*Nyaya Sastra*) it is stated that when we observe one cause for an happening, by inference we apply to the same happening at another place: "Wherever it is smoke, there is fire as we see in the kitchen; there is fire on the mountain as it is full of smoke (*Yatra yatra dhumas tatra tatra vahni yatha mahanase; parvato vahniman dhumavatvat*).

As the saying goes "there is a cause for everything". The great scientist Albert Einstein who discovered the theory of relativity and had died in 1955; it is quite hilarious to know that the scientists at Canada's McMaster University are trying to attribute his genius to the rare shape of his brain–its parietal lobe–which occupies the upper part of the back of the head–was more developed and atleast 15 per cent wider than the other brains it was compared with. This area of the brain is responsible for mathematical thought and processing space and movement. The other key difference which they found is that Einstein's brain misses a groove that normally runs along the temporal lobe which is involved in functions like speech and hearing development and separates it from the parietal lobes.[2] The critics, however, have put a caution to such explanation of complexity of the neural connections as till recently it was believed that intelligence was a function of brain size for which Einstein's brain was no exception. It is not clear that how these rich connections lead to a superior thought. "Until that is clear, there will be only correlations to go by, and many, many theories. And somewhere out there, one suspects, God will be laughing."[3] Any explanation based on the certain features of the head would only create another myth which should not be believed till we can verify the effects of functioning of the inter-connections of the features beyond doubt. Let us get familiar with the theory of causation as given by Carveth Read[4] before we get into the discussion on the causation in history.

1. That one thing is a mark of another and the surest of all marks is a cause.
2. The uniformity of space and time is involved in causation. If space and time were not uniform, causation would be irregular; for time and space are not agents, though they are conditions of every agent's operation.
3. A cause is relative to a given phenomenon, called the effect.
4. The given phenomenon is always an *event;* that is to say, not a new thing (nothing is wholly new), but a change in something or in the relative position of things.
5. The cause is antecedent to the effect, which is often called its *consequent.* Nor must it be supposed that the whole cause is antecedent to the effect as a whole.
6. The cause is tne *invariable* antecedent of the effect; that is to say, whenever a given cause occurs it always has the same effect; not every antecedent of an event is its cause but every event has an infinite number of antecedents that have no ascertainable connection with it. At the same time, if we consider the

antecedent state and process of things very widely and minutely, it never does exactly recur. If we consider the law of causation too strictly, it will render it inapplicable not only in practice but also in scientific inquiry.

7. The case is the Unconditional Antecedent that is the group of conditions (state and process of things) which, without any further condition (any necessary factor of a cause) is followed by the event in question: it is the least antecedent that suffices, positive conditions being present and negative absent.

8. That the cause of an event is an Immediate Antecedent follows from its being an unconditional one.

   A "remote cause" is doubly conditional; first because it supposes an intervening cause; and secondly, because it only in part determines the conditions that constitute this intervening cause.

The immediacy of a cause is implied in its unconditionalness, it is often so important a clue to it as to deserve a separate mention. Between the event and what seems to us the immediate antecedent, many things (molecular changes) may happen (say) in chemistry. And where phenomena are treated upon a large scale, as in the biological and social sciences, immediacy, as a mark of causation, must be liberally interpreted. So far, then, as to the qualitative character of Causation.

9. As to its quantitative character; as to the matter contained, and as to the energy embodied, cause and effect are conceived to be equal. The comprehension of the quantitative aspect of causation is greatly aided by analysis of any cause into a "Moving Power" and a "Collocation" of circumstances. When a demagogue, by making a speech stirs up a mob to a riot, the speech is the moving or inciting power; the mob already in a state of smouldering passion, and street convenient to be wrecked, are the collocation.

The cause of any event then, when exactly ascertainable has five marks: it is (quantitatively) *equal* to the effects, and is (qualitatively) its *immediate, unconditional, invariable antecedent.*

This scientific conception of causation, however has been developed and rendered definite by the investigations of the physical sciences that can avail themselves of exact experiments and mathematical calculation, and it is there, in chemistry, optics, thermotics and dynamics, that is most completely applicable. The conception can indeed be carried into Biological and Social Sciences, even in its quantitative form, by making the proper allowances.

Whenever, mental action is involved, there is a special difficulty in applying the physical notion of causation. For, clearly, if a cause is conceived as a matter in motion, a thought or feeling, or volition can be neither cause nor effect. And since mental action is involved in all social affairs, and in the life of men and animals, it may seem impossible to interpret social or vital changes according to laws of causation. Still, animals and men are moving bodies and it is recognised that their thoughts and feelings are so connected with their movements and with the movements of other things acting upon them, that we can judge one cause by another; although the connection is by no means well understood, and the best words (such as all can agree to use) have not yet been found to express even what we know about it.

In practical affairs, it is felt that everything depends upon causation, how to play the fiddle or sail a yacht, or get one's living, or defeat the enemy; practical affairs call for promptitude and decisive seizing upon what is predominantly important. These prompt and decisive judgements as to what is the cause, or predominantly important condition, of any event, are not as good as a scientific estimate of all the conditions, when this can be obtained; but when time is short, the insight of trained sagacity may be much better than an imperfect theoretical treatment of such problems.

We should also consider concurrent consequences of any cause, may be called co-effects: the effect being the sum of them. We should enlarge our views of the consequences of any cause. An important consequence of eating is to satisfy hunger, and this is the ordinary motive to eat, but for health and strength some sorts are much better than others. An important consequences of firing a gun is the propulsion of the bullet or shell, but there are many other consequences in the whole effect, and one of them is the heating of the gun, which, accumulating with rapid firing, may at last put the gun out of action.

The neglect to take account of the whole effect (that is, of all the co-effects) in any cause of causation is perhaps the reason why many philosophers have maintained the doctrine of a "Plurality of Causes" : meaning not that more than one condition is operative in the antecedent of every event (which is true), but the same event may be due at different times to different antecedents, that in fact there may be *vicarious* causes.

As we are far from knowing events minutely, it is necessary in practical affairs, and even in the more complex and unmanageable scientific investigations, especially those that deal with human life, to acknowledge a possible plurality of causes for any effect. Indeed, forgetfulness of this leads to many rash generalisations; as that 'revolutions always begin in hunger' or that 'myths are a disease of language'. A scientific method recognizes that there may be other causes of effects thus vaguely conceived, and then proceeds to distinguish in each class of effects, the peculiarities due to different causes.

The understanding of the complex nature of causes and effects helps us to overcome some other difficulties that perplex the use of the these words. We have seen that the true cause is an *immediate* antecedent; but if the cause is confounded with *one* of its constituent conditions, it may seem to have long preceded the event which is regarded as its effect. Thus if one man's death is ascribed to another's desire of revenge, this desire may have been entertained for years before the assassination occurred; similarly, if a shipwreck is ascribed to a sunken reef, the rock was waiting for ages before the ship sailed that way. But, of course, neither the desire of revenge nor the sunken rock was 'the sum of conditions' on which the one or the other event depended. The true effect of any state or process of things is the immediate consequence.

When a cause consists of two or more conditions or forces, we may consider what effect any one of them would have if it operated alone, that is to say, its *tendency*. Again considering the tendency of any force, if it is operated alone, we may say that, when combined with another force (not in the same direction) in any resultant, its tendency is *counteracted* either partially or wholly.

The several conditions constituting any cause, then by aiding or counteracting one another's tendencies, jointly determine the total effect. Hence, viewed in relation to one another, they may be said to stand is *reciprocity* or mutual influence.[5]

We also observe that when cause disappears, the effect also vanishes. When a machinery is malfunctioning or stops working, after the mechanical or electronic repairs, it resumes its normal function. Similarly in human affairs, as a story goes that how an unhappy family was transformed into a trouble-free family. A mother was questioned by her children why the father cries aloud and creates a panic situation in the family? The mother brought round the children stating: "Mark when your father cries: either when you get up late, or quarrel with each other or get late to the school. You stop this and father will stop crying". The children corrected their ways and the family became a happy family.

There is no mono-causal explanation in history given by historians while assigning causes to events, but multiplicity of causes–economic, political, ideological, social and personal causes, including long-term and short-term factors. Carr simplifies the answer for outbreak of Russian Revolution in 1917 from examination point of view–stating that if the examination candidate while answering the question offered only one cause, he will be lucky to get a third class; the second candidate who tries to offer simply a dozen causes one after the other for the Russian Revolution, might get a second class, but scarcely a first – it being , probably well informed, but unimaginative answer. The true historian with his list of causes would first reduce it to order and try to establish some hierarchy of causes, fixing their relation to one another, attempting to explain which cause or which category of causes, should be regarded 'in the last resort "or" the final analysis' (favourite phrases of historians) as the ultimate cause, of all causes.[6] According to E.H. Carr the causes of the Bolshevik Revolution may be enumerated as Russia's successive military defeats, the collapse of the Russian economy under pressure of war, the effective propaganda of the Bolsheviks, the failure of the Tsarist government to solve the agrarian problem, the concentration of an impoverished and exploited proletariat in the factories of Petrograd[7], of them we may place up the leadership of Lenin.

Similarly, we have many causes and different interpretations by different historians on all the important events – be it the French Revolution[8], or causes of the 'Puritan Revolution' in the seventeenth century England or the causes of the American Revolution[9], or the Origins of the First World War or the Second World War[10].

When we come down to Indian history, we also find the plurality of reasons assigned as causes whether it is the Decline of the Mauryas or the fall of the Gupta Empire or the decline of the Mughal Empire.

Romila Thapar outlines the causes for the decline of the Mauryas to various causes such as the succession of weak kings, partition of the Empire, Greek invasions of the North–West though some historians have blamed the pacifist policy of Ashoka while Haraprasad Sastri had seen it as a result of the Brahmanical revolution while Kosambi alludes it to considerable pressure on the Mauryan economy under the later Mauryas.[11]

Professor Thapar states as follows :

> "The decline of the Mauryan Empire cannot be satisfactorily explained by quoting military inactivity, brahman resentment, popular uprisings, or economic pressure. The causes were far more fundamental and included a much wider perspective of Mauryan life than any of those mentioned above. Further more, the decline of other empires and periods of political expansion, may also be explained in part by these same reasons. The organization of administration, and the conception of the state or the nation, were of great significance in the causes of the decline of the Mauryas."[12]

Similarly, it is worth noticing what Majumdar, while concluding on the fall of the Gupta empire, said : "Inspite of the many uncertain factors in the history of the period, the above review will make it clear that the Huna invasion cannot be regarded as the chief cause of the downfall of the empire. It no doubt operated as an important contributory factor, but the internal dissensions in the imperial family, the ambitious enterprise of Yasodharman and the assertion of independence by feudal vassals and provincial governors were mainly instrumental in bringing about its collapse... The decline and downfall of the Gupta Empire was brought about by the same causes which operated in the case of the Maurya empire in the older and the Mughal empire in later days."[13]

The decline of the Mughal empire has also been interpreted differently by different historians. While Irfan Habib ascribes it to the Agrarian unrest, Satish Chandra assigns the main reason as the crisis of the Jagirdari system while some others assign it to the repressive and anti-Hindu policies of the emperor Aurangzeb. Sometimes in spite of individual reasons things do not take place in certain groups because of the lack of sufficient social conditions. Durkheim's study of suicide is a case in example. Durkheim found out that the rate of suicides varied between different social groups inspite of individual reasons being the same. The married Catholics living in a settled village community were found less prone to suicide in comparison to the Protestants who singly lived in towns where there is much social mobility. Thus Durkheim could account for variations in the rate of suicide between different places. Thus social scientists and historians can identify social causes for certain tendencies such as suicide but frequently do not take place due to intervening circumstances.[14]

Thus we see that though the human nature is basically the same as stated by David Hume, the trajectory is different in each human action. Hume emphasised on the uniformity of human nature:

> "It is universally acknowledged that there is a great uniformity among the actions of men, in all nations and ages, and that human nature remains still the same in its principles and operations. The same motives always produce the same actions; the same events follow from the same causes. Ambition, avarice, self-love, vanity, friendship, generosity, public spirit–these passions, mixed in various degrees and distributed through society, have been, from the beginning of the World, and still are , the source of all the actions and enterprises which have been observed among mankind."[15]

Hume's basic science was largely suppositional–there is no long-term recurrence or regular connection in human phenomena. Hence Collingwood argued, we do not have that degree of likeness in the thoughts and deeds of agents at various times in history sufficient to allow for any universal laws: accordingly the trans-historical generalization, which we find in general laws is in principle impossible.[16]

We may also observe that human intentions play a very important role in human action. In the law, a man is punishable more for his intention to kill a person when proved so than when a person got killed by accident.

According to Wittgenstein, an intention is not a physical thing or mental event to be examined. Rather it is a way of interpreting the behaviour of an animal or a person in a certain context. It is a way of talking about them, a kind of language game.[17] It shows us how the act was warranted, given the actor, his social and physical situation and his beliefs and wants. It has also been observed that people do not act on their intentions due to their inherent nature or other forces, pressures, constraints and modify or change their intentions and even form new intentions. Hence, we need not formulate a deterministic theory of the mind.[18] We may agree with McCullagh that reasons do influence people and sometimes powerfully but with a difference that reasons can be causes for change of the intentions of human beings. Further it is not necessary that the human beings change their intentions, sometimes they may strengthen their intentions with the forces behind them. As we have noticed from Read's theory of Causation, the human-beings move from one place to another, in case they have not acted instantly on their emotion or intention, they may discuss the matter with others or review it by themselves and modify, change or strengthen their intention accordingly.

Reacting to the theory of "Determinism in History" and simultaneously the theory of "Historical Inevitability", Carr states that determinism is a problem not of history but of all human behaviour. "That every thing that happens has a cause or causes, and could not have happened differently unless something in the cause or causes had also been different."[19] Carr draws our attention to some intervening factors which change the usual behaviour of a person on a particular day or moment and exhorts historians to avoid the use of such strong expressions for some occurrence as "inevitable" which may only indicate that the conjunction of factors leading to the event was overwhelmingly strong. Carr prefers to use the expression "extremely probable" in such cases.[20] However, we may say that events take their own course under the circumstances. Once they have taken place, they were 'inevitable' since the factors to delay or stop the event were absent. Or in Carr's words: "for it have happened otherwise, the antecedent causes would have had to be different."[21]

We may also consider the role of chance or accident in history. In the sequence of events, if an accident plays a vital role then it is relevant and significant. The role of accident is unique and hence it cannot be generalised. It involves value judgements and is related to the teleological view of history. Even Marx accepts the role of chance in history and specifies the 'chance' character of the individuals who are at the head of a movement at the outset.[22] Antony's infatuation with Cleopatra (especially Cleopatra's nose), the pet monkey's bite that killed king Alexander of Greece in the autumn of 1920 or the death of Lenin, were mere accidents which modified the course of history.[23] Since "they were accidental, they do not enter into any rational interpretation of history, or into the historian's hierarchy of significant causes."[24]

We also learn from the British History that "God blew with the wind and the Armeda was ruined". Similarly, it is difficult to explain the role of catastrophes, floods, cyclones, famines and big accidents in the life of people who get affected. "History begins with the handling down of tradition; and tradition means the carrying of the habits and lessons of the past into the future."[25] –writes Carr while commenting on the interpretation in history which is bound up with value judgements.

The big accidents, floods, famines etc. may have a cause but largely the people in a country with strong religions tradition see the Invisible hand (God) punishing the people for their accumulated sins. In India, we have a strong literary tradition of explaining events with remote causes. The violation of the law of primogeniture by Santanu and ascending the throne, ignoring his elder brother Devapi in the Kuru dynasty resulted in drought in the king's reign for a period of twelve years. Similarly Lord Rama was born as a son to Dasaratha to suffer in forests, for fourteen years for arranging a mockery on devarshi Narada by Lord Vishnu (Lord Rama being an incarnation) where Lord Hanuman served him in the form of a monkey, which form Lord Vishnu had given to Narada to participate in a *Svayamvara* (marriage by choice). By another curse, King Dasaratha was to suffer and die suffering the pangs of separation of his son Rama as by accident he had killed son, Sravana Kumar, who was serving his blind parents and had come to the tank to fill up a jar of water for them. We also know how sixty thousands sons of king Sagara were cursed to die in flames by sage Kapil on account of their, misbehaviour to him and who were later purified by the great penance of their grandson Bhagiratha who was instrumental in bringing the Ganges to this earth.[26] The whole Indian Epic and Puranic literature is replete with such examples where the curse and the boon serve as the causative factors. Whether these events actually occurred or not we can have no evidence to verify them. Even if they are believed to be 'myths' which are deemed to be 'half truths' – they convey a meaning and are deemed to be the carriers of value system in the society.

Notes

1. E.H. Carr, *What is History?*, p. 87
2. *The New Indian Express,* Hyderabad, June 19, 1999, p. 11.
3. *Ibid.,* June 21, 1999, p. 10.
4. Carveth Read, *Logic,* pp., 168 – 184.
5. *Ibid.,* p. 184.
6. E.H. Carr, *op. cit.* pp., 89 – 90.
7. *Ibid.* p. 89
8. Marwick, *The Nature of History* , pp. 57 – 77; McCullagh, *The Truth of History,* pp. 87 – 88,
9. Marwick, *op. cit.,* pp. 223 – 227.

10. *Ibid.*, pp. 235 – 239.
11. Romila Thapar, *Asoka and the Decline of the Mauryas,* OUP, revised edition, Delhi, 1997, pp. 197 – 206.
12. *Ibid.*, p. 207.
13. R.C. Majumdar & A.S. Altekar, *The Vakataka – Gupta Age,* Delhi, Reprinted 1986, pp. 217 – 218.
14. McCullagh, *op. cit.*, pp. 263 – 264.
15. *Inquiry,* pp. 92 –93, as quoted in Rex Martin, *Historical Explanation*, Corwell University Press, London 1997, p. 25
16. Martin, *op. cit.*, pp. 29 –31.
17. McCullagh, *op. cit.*, p. 238.
18. *Ibid.*, pp. 237 – 239.
19. E.H. Carr, *op. cit.* P. 93.
20. *Ibid.*, p. 96.
21. *Ibid.*
22. *Ibid.*, p. 101.
23. *Ibid.*, pp. 98 – 103.
24. *Ibid.*, p. 103.
25. *Ibid.*, pp. 107 –108.
26. T.R. Sharma, *The Concept of History,* pp. 77 – 82.

8

OBJECTIVITY IN HISTORY

An individual lives in society and is a social being; being born in a family, inherits the traits of his family and environment of his society, country and ideology. Thus an individual is supposed to have some predilection of family/lineage, social status, race, region, religion and culture. Objectivity is a quality of mind which varies from person to person in degree to be successful in rising above the predilection to race, religion and culture as an observer, participant and author or narrator of historical events such as wars, rebellions and revolutions. It has been found that the individual behaviour varies individually but is quite different when an individual is a part of group, mob or crowd. Even individually, he is constrained to behave in a certain way as he wishes due to various pulls, pressures and values enshrined in the society of which he forms a part himself. Hence it is not easy to find a person who will give a dispassionate, detached and neutral view of the happenings and will not exhibit any bias or prejudice in his writings. That is why Kalhana, the author of the *Rajatarangini* or 'River of Kings" a chronicler of the kings of Kashmir (A. D. 1148) stated that a historian should try, as best as possible, to act as a judge, who tries to examine the case on the basis of the evidence before him. Aware of his built-in biases and prejudices, he must try to overcome them while collecting and evaluating the evidence pertaining to his subject.[1]

Secondly, in natural sciences a scientist himself works on his data and conducts the experiment which can be replicated for observation and verification by himself or others as the case may be. But in human affairs, the incidents, accidents, wars, revolts and revolutions cannot be repeated. Even the evidence–oral or documentary which is provided with the historian is likely to be subjective as it is given by an observer who may be subject to all his prejudices and predilections. Again it is reviewed by the historian who may not be entirely free from all biases and prejudices due to him as an individual. This leaves very little scope for objectivity in history. The aim of all objective knowledge is to reach the truth, hence in social sciences, we can reach very approximation to the truth but not the truth.

It has been opined that if we follow scientific method we can write objective history. John Passmore writes that since the events which concern the historian are *past*, they cannot be data, but must always be inferences or reconstructions: "The natural scientist, it is argued, can always pass beyond the recorded facts to the facts themselves, and this direct reference to the facts is the essence of objectivity; the scientist confronts the world as it nakedly is, whereas the historian sees it, always, through the medium of someone else's testimony–a testimony he can never by the nature of the case penetrate beyond, because the events the testimony describes are gone for ever.[2]

Passmore further states that even if we compare history with sciences like Astronomy and Seismology: the testimony on which scientist has to rely is the careful recording of a fact by a trained observer; the historian, on the other hand, begins with chronicles i.e. with testimonies composed by someone who had an axe to grind. The so-called "sources" of history, wrote Popper in *The Open Society* only record such facts as appeared sufficiently interesting to record, so that sources will contain only facts, that fit in with a preconceived theory.[3]

We may state that the historians are conscious of this fact about the sources as L. B. Kenny states: "The problem of writing history is overcome not by hugging the sources too closely but by getting behind them and by seeking and expounding the underlying situations reflected in them. Utilising the sources applying the best of available techniques and making out a case adequately supported by evidence, is the main function of a historian. History, after all is a rational account of man's activities based on scientific criticism of the sources".[4]

However, Passmore refutes the charge by L. B Namier that history is necessarily subjective and individual, conditioned by the interest and the vision of the historian as the historian is selective of his enquiry by regarding certain facts as unimportant and others as important. Passmore states that "every form of enquiry is selective even in sciences as a physicist is interested only in such physical operations as bear upon a problem he is investigating; a historian similarly will refer only to those facts which in some way bear upon the story he is telling"[5]. He calls historical problem akin to applied science than the problems in pure science. The historian is interested in what happens in a particular situation on a particular occasion; just as an engineer may have to ask himself: "Why did that aeroplane collapse? So the historian asks: "Why did that monarchy collapse?". "Like the engineer, the historian constructs a narrative model, say, the collapse of the monarchy in France, to the strains and stresses which were relevant to that collapse. He may comment well, bidding us to pay special attention to this or that point in his narrative.[6] Still Passmore rightly comments: "The most that can be said against history, then, is that there is *sometimes* no known way of deciding between conflicting historical hypotheses; this difficulty is not peculiar to history and ought not to be alleged against its objectivity".[7]

Finally, Passmore states that we do not fix a very hard criterion of objectivity in history to see every work on history as a final and finished product on the theme, history edges its way in with the rest of the disciplines as such unanimity is not to be found in any branch of human inquiry. He cites the conflicting views on the French Revolution in different history books which need not really be in conflict with one another; each reflects a different aspect of the revolution.[8]

McCullagh while commenting on the objectivity of descriptive explanations cautions us about the use of some general terms being used in history such as 'revolution' or ' class-struggle'. For example the question "what was the French Revolution like?" This is an example of the general concept which the historian has in mind. Explanations are generally judged if they provide all the information requested. We may objectively judge whether the description of a subject does exemplify the general concepts of that subject or it does not. Occasionally the meaning of a general concept is drawn from a social theory, such as a Marxist theory of revolution, or an economic theory of society. In that case, the historian must indicate the sense in which the term is being used for the people to judge the adequacy of the descriptive explanation which is governed by it. If a preconception does not fit the facts, it is false. "It was wrong to describe the English Civil War as a class struggle because the opposing sides did not represent distinct classes".[9]

McCullagh comments that where there are several possible meanings of a general term to choose from, historians are more likely to choose one which reflects their interests. In that case, the consequent descriptive explanation can be said to be subjective, in as much as it is designed to exemplify a concept chosen for personal reasons. "In practice, as has been seen, descriptive explanations have been most criticized for being either untrue or unfair. Unfairness can be difficult to detect when a whole community of scholars shares a particular bias. It is notorious that historians up until a generation ago overlooked the history of indigenous people in lands settled by Europeans; overlooked the history of women and children; found it difficult to understand the point of view of their country's enemies. Communal bias is the most difficult to guard against".[10]

Commenting on the objectivity of historical interpretations, McCullagh quotes Charles A. Beard, an American historian who had presented in An Economic Interpretation of the constitution of the United States, questioned the objectivity in history on the following three grounds:

(1) Any overarching hypothesis or conception employed to give coherence and structure to past events in written history is an interpretation of some kind, something transcendent;

(2) Second , since an interpretation does not refer to anything that was really there, it cannot be true or false; and

(3) Third, in Beard's opinion the source of an interpretation is the historian herself: Into the selection of topics, the choice and arrangement of materials, specific historian "me" will enter.

The historian's choice will reflect his 'time, place, circumstance, interests, predilections, culture'.[11]

McCullagh, however, does not support the contention of Beard stating there is nothing wrong with bringing in concepts for understanding the past. General descriptions if they satisfy truth conditions and are not misleading, they can be true and fair. The same subject can have equally well, several different interpretations. The important question is that–are the historians so biased that they cannot rationally consider whether the interpretation is true, fair or good?[12] Finally he is optimistic to state that they assiduously criticize existing interpretations in these regards and seek better ones to replace them. He quotes the example of Christopher Hill who first interpreted the English Civil War with Marxist assumptions in 1955, though three years later in 1958 he accepted that such an interpretation was not a good one and preferred a synthetic approach to the subject so as to have a wider understanding of the problem.[13]

We may quote Weber in this context who states that "The *objective* validity of all empirical knowledge rests exclusively upon the ordering of the given reality according to categories which are *subjective* in a specific sense, namely in that they present the *presuppositions* of our knowledge and are based on the presupposition of the *value* of those *truths* which empirical knowledge is able to give us.... In the empirical social sciences, as we have seen the possibility of meaningful knowledge of what is essential for us in the infinite richness of events is bound up with the unremitting application of viewpoints of a specifically particularised character, which in the last analysis, are oriented on the basis of evaluative ideas. These evaluative ideas are for their part empirically discoverable and analyzable as elements of meaningful human conduct, but their validity *cannot* be deduced from empirical data as such. The "objectivity" of the social sciences depends rather on the fact that the empirical data are related to these evaluative ideas which alone make them worth knowing and the significance of the empirical data is derived from these evaluative ideas".[14]

Dr. Devahuti states that "the essential matter of history is not what happened but what people felt about what happened. That is the reality of the times. It is of little consequence whether we think it was ugly, beautiful or indifferent".[15]

It were the British, who in modern India, sought to investigate the heritage of India and laid the foundations of Indian history in the modern approach to historical writing. The British projected India of the eighteenth century in a horrible condition and tried to explain it by the theory of oriental despotism to serve their interest as rulers created a theory of benevolent despotism. Another theory of Aryan race was given birth to justify the foreign rule in India, that the coming of the English represented 'a reunion of parted cousins, the descendants of two different families of ancient Aryan race'[16] which gave rise to lot of distortions in Indian history.

The British plagued the writing of Indian history with so many biases and prejudices to serve their imperial interests on communal and cultural divide, to achieve their ends by following the policy of divide and rule. James Mill who first published the *History of British India* in 1918 divided Indian history into three civilizations, the Hindu, the Muslim and the British[17]. Mill assumed the superiority of the British over India and its past. He indicated Indian society and advocated the use of power and law to revolutionise it.[18]

Indian nationalist historians, on the other hand, did not take such criticisms lying down and refuted such by glorifying Indian social institutions and Indian history. Hinduism, was defended in its entirety, and certain of its ardent advocates even asserted its supremacy over other religions. Social abuses, such as the caste system were either denied or diluted or rationalised. Even *Sati* was in some ways glorified. The British regime was denounced as rooted in tyranny and exploitation; their military successes were attributed either to treachery, forgery or bribery. They emphasised democracy and pride in the culture of the past.[19] Thus we may state that both the imperial and nationalist historiographies may not stand the tests of time and it is required to write a new history by reviewing the evidence without any bias or prejudice. Another fallacy which was created by the British was that Indians had no sense of history: Indians were a-historical people and kept no records of their history and that Indian society was a static society, disallowing any change in their social institutions and economic foundations. Such myths or fallacies have been exploded by the historians of modern India.[20]

We need to study both the economic forces operating in society and economy as well as the ideological framework to understand historical reality. This synthetic approach can help us in confirming the reality as derived from other sources. "Historical explanation then becomes an enterprise in which the refinements of concepts and theories are a constant necessity, not only because of the availability of fresh evidence from new sources but also because of greater precision in our understanding of the categories which we use to analyse these sources".[21]

In the post-independence India, in the earlier decades, there has been a proliferation of studies with Marxist approach to Indian history. These studies helped in some way for the perception of social reality but ignored some other important aspects of social reality from the point of view of ideology prevalent in the contemporary society. They over-emphasised the role of economic forces to the neglect of ideological forces. Sometimes even they closed their eyes to the other rational explanations since it did not suit their ideal. It has invited criticism from other section of historians:

"The Marxist approach too is both unscientific and unhistorical. Marx certainly did a great service to the understanding of history by emphasising the part played by economic factors. He thereby showed the inadequacy of understanding a people and their history on the basis of religion, literature or political system to the exclusion of their economic system. It is true that one does not live by bread alone but it is truer that one cannot live without bread. The material life of the common people, their economic and technological progress, the class controlling the economic power – all these certainly mould a country's history and culture. But the Marxist mistake lies in overdoing this. The place of individual in the history of a Napolean, a Buddha or, on Asoka cannot be underestimated. Today, even some Marxists concede that "heroes" are important in the crucial moments of Historical Divides. The Marxist approach emphasising the materialist aspects of civilization has led them to glorify the Kushana age and underplay the Gupta age on the basis of discoveries of relatively poor architecture in the Gupta strata compared to the Kushana strata. Against this, it may be pointed out that some monuments of the Gupta period like the Devgarh temple, the Aphsad temple and others do not prove architectural decay. Anyhow, the critical point is that over-emphasis on material excellence or decay does not do proper justice to any civilization at any point of time. Culture is not only agriculture and architecture. The literary, educational, religious and philosophical outpourings of the Gupta Age freed from the trammels of foreign strings place it on a much higher pedestal than the Kushana. The obsession with one type of source led Woolly, absolutely wrongly, to characterise Vedic civilization as barbaric. The Marxist approach is basically inadequate and often mischievous in seeing one to the exclusion of the many truths of history".[22]

Even Irfan Habib informs us that "It is inherent in the unity of past and present that Marxist historiography must continuously turn to fresh aspects to explore and re-explore and seek fresh questions to answer".[23]

Prof. Habib mentions the text book view of Marxism as 'determinism'. While Marxists have protested against this characterization, their own description of 'Historical Materialism' (as in Stalin's essay *Dialectical and Historical Materialism*) is often in fact couched in deterministic terms. We are told that the production of technology ('forces of production') determines the social relationships ('relations of production'). These together constitute the 'mode of production', which determines the World of ideas and culture ('the superstructure'). For has not Marx said, "It is their social being that determines their consciousness'. Clearly the relationship of technique–class relations and mode of production–and culture, is crucial, but in what way exactly one part of relationship 'determine' the configuration of the other part?"[24]. He rebuts the idea of a universal feudal system as it would go strikingly against the law of uneven development which is so vital a part of Marxist dialectics. He writes, "All social formations contain contradictions; the most important revolve around classes and express themselves in the form of class struggles. For Marxist historians it is not only important to rescue from oblivion the narratives of rebellions of the subjugated classes but also to analyse their nature and the extent to which their participants were aware of their true class affiliations. For there can be class struggles without the participants realizing that they are such. Unfortunately, since many of the uprisings are written about by their opponents, who were partisans of the ruling classes, we have often no means of knowing what the rebels really thought. Even so, one becomes aware that there was more class consciousness in the peasant rebellions of China or in England in 1881 than in the agrarian uprisings in India of the seventeenth century. The reasons for this backwardness, such as possibly the caste system, must be investigated; these may well have lessons for us to-day".[25] Thus Prof. Habib points out the shortfalls in Marxian analysis and reminds us to perceive and understand the social reality from Marxian point of view, with a clear vision.

Another school of historical analysis which has emerged in 1970s and hereafter is the 'Subaltern School'. Irfan Habib, as a critic of this School remarks that Ranajit Guha, and other scholars of the 'subaltern school' who use Gramsci's terminology (but in a peculiar way and with additions like 'elite classes'), lay particular stress on the 'autonomy' of the 'subaltern classes' in ideology and culture. He states: "Their 'subaltern classes 'however, often appear to be not true classes, but merely castes, tribes and communities, where *Zamindars* and peasants are seen and accepted as undifferentiated. The view that these composite groups necessarily developed 'autonomous' ideologies (as the working class does in Marxism) is an unproven premise".[26]

At another place, Prof. Habib also severely criticizes the subaltern approach to the National Movement. He charges that their historical perspective is unacceptably narrow, by stating that the mobilization in the domain of elite politics was achieved vertically whereas in that of subaltern politics this was achieved horizontally. Prof. Habib writes; "Indeed, Gramsci, from whose manuscript writings the term 'subaltern' has been taken, denied that the peasantry can have an ideology created by itself, or that it can have its own intelligentsia. The nature of mass struggles changed qualitatively as well as quantitatively once the National Movement came on the scene ......It can be argued that the self-perception of the peasants as a class was itself made possible or perceptibly deepened by the National Movement, just as peasant unrest was an important factor fuelling the latter."[27]

Same is true for the nationalist historiography. We echo the words of Jadunath Sarkar who stated: "I would not care whether truth is pleasant or unpleasant and in consonance with or opposed to current views. I would not mind in the least whether truth is or is not blow to the glory of my country. If necessary, I shall bear in patience the ridicule and slander of friends and society for the sake of preaching truth. But still I shall seek truth, understand truth and accept truth. This should be the firm resolve of a historian."[28] Later Jadunath wrote in 1937 to Dr. Rajendra Prasad when asked to serve as a chief editor to a comprehensive national history of India: "National history, like every other history worthy of the name and deserving to endure, must be true as regards the facts and reasonable in the interpretation of them ......".[29] To which Dr. Rajendra Prasad wrote, "I entirely agree with you that no history is worth the name which suppresses or distorts facts. A historian who purposely does so under the impression that he thereby does good to his native country really harms it in the end. Much more so, in the case of a country like ours which has suffered much on account of its national defects, and which must know and understand them to be able to remedy them."[30]

We remain with an open mind to all such approaches to Indian history whether Nationalist, Marxist or subaltern by name, but somebody will some day point out the lack of accuracy in the presentation of facts or where the explanation or interpretation crosses the limits of rationale or probability. And the dialogue will continue to seek the truth.

Notes

1. B.P. Sinha "The Redundancies and the Lacunae in Indian Historiography" in Devahuti (ed.) *Problems of Indián Historiography,* Delhi, 1979, p. 99.
2. John Passmore, "The Objectivity of History" in Patrick Gardiner (ed.) *The Philosophy of History,* OUP, London, 1974 reprinted 1984, pp. 147-148.

3. *Ibid.*, p. 149.
4. L.B. Kenny, "Problems of Historical Writing in India with Reference to The History of the Deccan" in S. Gopal and R. Thapar, *Problems of Historical Writing in India,* New Delhi, 1963, p. 24.
5. Passmore, *op cit.*, pp. 151-152.
6. *Ibid.*, pp. 153 – 155.
7. *Ibid.*, p. 155.
8. *Ibid.*, pp. 158 –159.
9. McCullagh, *The Truth of History*, p. 109.
10. *Ibid.*, pp. 109 –110.
11. *Ibid.*, p. 130 as quoted.
12. *Ibid.*, p. 131.
13. *Ibid.*, pp. 131-133.
14. Max Weber, *The Methodology of the Social Sciences,* New York, 1949, pp. 110-111.
15. Devahuti, "Notes on Approaches to Indian History" in Devahuti (ed.) *op. cit.*, p. 92.
16. Romila Thapar, *Interpreting Early India,* pp. 1-22.
17. Romila Thapar, *op. cit.*, p. 89.
18. D.P Singhal, "Battle For the Past" in Devahuti (ed.); *op. cit.*, p. 153.
19. *Ibid.*, p. 158.
20. Romila Thapar, *The Past and Prejudice,* New Delhi, 1973 *Passim.*; *Interpreting Early India, Passim.*
21. Romila Thapar, *Interpreting Early India,* p. 136.
22. B.P Sinha, "The Redundancies and the Lacunae in Indian Historiography" in Devahuti (ed.) *Problems of Indian Historiography,* pp. 98-99. Also see Rasesh Jamindar, "The Concept of the Golden Age and Some General Problems" in the same work, pp. 76-77.
23. Irfan Habib, *Essays in Indian History : Towards a Marxist Perception,* New Delhi, 1995, p.1.
24. *Ibid.*, pp. 2-3.
25. *Ibid.*, pp. 6-7.
26. *Ibid.*, p. 7.
27. Irfan Habib, *Interpreting Indian History,* pp. 58-59.
28. R.C Majumdar, *Historiography in Modern India,* Bombay, 1970, p. 56 as quoted.
29. *Ibid.*
30. *Ibid.*, *A New History of the Indian People,* Vol. VI. pp. vi – vii. as quoted.

9

FOOTNOTES AND BIBLIOGRAPHY

The Manner of Footnotes

The footnotes are a necessary requirement in a thesis or research work. They endorse the statements made by the author and help the reader to identify the sources used by the author. They authenticate the work of the author as well as acknowledge the contribution made by other scholars in the field. They may refer to a citation by an author or an abridgement of the statements of an author and may spell out the source or the agent of the information. They satisfy the curiosity of the reader over a statement which seems to the normally unusual. They help us to tap the original source and consult in detail to settle a dispute over the meaning or inference drawn by the scholars.

The footnotes are given at the bottom of the page so as not to obstruct the main argument or the dialogue being carried on in the work. They are also required to elaborate certain terms or to represent different views by the other scholars over some concepts which cannot find space in the main body of the thesis but certainly need to be treated in a fair manner. Sometimes, if they need more space than usually required they may be put as Appendix or Appendices in the end of the work. Mainly the footnotes serve two purposes : to relieve the text of the obscure material and to quote the source of information for the statements made in the text. There is no universally accepted method for writing reference footnotes hence some publishers, institutions or Editors prescribe their own norms for submission of books, articles, reviews etc. for publication for the sake of uniformity or style. Moreover, we also find variation of style in usage by different social science subjects at least. The footnotes, as the name indicates were in the beginning only given at the bottom of the page. But slowly and steadily the scholars or publication houses have created some conventions as matters of convenience as well as to continue the flow of the author for the reader's eye not to distract its attention from it. Some footnotes being lengthy, created the problem of adjustment of space for the typist or the printer; they are given at the end of each chapter with the heading: *Footnotes* or *Notes and References* in the ascending order of numericals. Sometimes even they are given in the end of the book chapter-wise.

The Method of Footnotes

"Footnotes must be clearly appropriated to the statement which they are supposed to support. This may mean that in a difficult passage every sentence or even every half-sentence, may have to have a reference number attached to it, which is very tiresome for the eyes of the reader; but in a dissertation, as opposed to a book, it is less important that the page should look elegant and attractive than that the evidence for the statements made should be clearly appropriated. The form and wording of the footnote must always make clear what statement the note is intended to establish and what books or paper it intends to cite."[1]

The footnotes can be given in a type-script in Arabic numerals in brackets indicated in the body of the thesis thus (1), (2), (3) in ascending order, indicating the name of the author in a straight manner, the name of the book, the place of publication, and the year of publication and the edition. The name of the book should be underlined. One should check up the edition and verify if one is borrowing the footnote from the other author about the page number, if the earlier author has used some different edition of the book. If by any means one is unable to verify it is advised to state 'as quoted'. If one wants to refer to some other works which show the same interpretation or with little variation, one may add *cf.*, (compare or see) and refer to the other related works under reference. In case of a singular reference it should be indicated in the following manner :

1. T.R. Sharma, The Concept of History, Delhi, 1987

When the succeeding reference is also to the same book or the same passage you may indicate that by *Ibid.*, (*ibidem,* in the same place). In case, the page number has changed, you may indicate that after *Ibid.* by specifying the other page number or numbers.

If you are repeatedly using the single work of an author in the nearby page, you may mention the first, the name of the author and then the conventional abbreviation *op.cit* (*opere citato,* in the work cited) and *loc. cit.* (*loco citato,* in the place cited). If such need arises at a quite distant page, the use of these abbreviations may be better avoided so as not to put the reader to a difficulty in hunting back to the original reference. It is even sometimes better to evolve a scheme of abbreviations by the author himself, which must be added as a *List of Abbreviations* to the dissertation and to use an abbreviated form of the full title.[2] Especially, you can make use of this technique if a different citation intervenes between the two notes.

In case of an article in an edited work, the title of the article should be placed within inverted commas and in the work it is published should be underlined as in the following example :

Romila Thapar, "Asokan India and the Gupta Age" in A.L. Basham (ed.) A Cultural History of India, Oxford University Press, Delhi, 1975, Tenth Impression, 1996, pp.38-50.

In case there are two editors, both the names should be mentioned and afterwards it should be indicated within brackets as (eds.) in place of (ed.).

In case there are more than two authors, it should be indicated as such after mention of the two names *et al.* (eds.)

If you are referring to a collection of documents, but first the name of the collection, then the volume number, and then the folio number of the first page of the document or the page where the quotation occurs, and lastly the description of the document.

In case the reference is made to the Government records which are printed, the name of the record should be underlined, date with year, volume number if any and the page number or page numbers be indicated.

If the document is a letter or letters which need to be catalogued, they are catalogued under the sender's (not the recipient) proper name and arranged in chronological order when they are received from the same writer. While referring to letter, it is normal to put the writer first, then the recipient, and then the date of writing and the place.

In case of a newspaper, the name of the newspaper should be underlined, date, year and page number be indicated. We are enclosing a chart of conventional abbreviations commonly used in the footnotes (see chart).

A : **Chart of Conventional Abbreviations (used in footnotes)**

Cf.	:	compare or see
Ch.; chap.	:	Chapter
C.U.P	:	Cambridge University Press
Ed.	:	Editor, Edited by
edn.	:	Edition
et al.	:	and others (of persons)
etc.	:	and so forth (of thing)
f.,ff.	:	and the following page (s)
Ibid.	:	(from latin *ibidem,* in the same place)
i.e.	:	that is
infra.	:	Below
ital.	:	Italics
loc. cit.	:	(From Latin *loco citato* in the place cited)
op. cit.	:	(From Latin *opere citato,* in the work cited)
O.U.P	:	Oxford University Press
p., pp.	:	page, pages
passim	:	here and there
supra	:	above
tr.	:	Translation
V, vol.	:	Volume
Viz.	:	namely

Caution: One must be careful in the use of the footnotes. It must be seen whether the material you are taking to the footnote should be part of the main argument then it should never be relegated to the footnote.

Secondly, one must be sure of the reference to be absolutely accurate. Sometimes, very adverse comments have come in the reports on the theses submitted by the candidates in respect of the footnotes with regard to their accuracy or suitability to the statements made in the body of the thesis. One must check, as far as possible, the footnotes with the originals to see that they are all right. One must consistently use the same edition of a book for the sake of accuracy and not copy from the other authors where it is likely they may have used a different edition which may change the page numbers or even modify or change the views of the author.

Bibliography

Objectives: The primary object of a bibliography is to show upon what evidence the dissertation is based. It should not be a bibliography swollen by the addition of the books which have no real relation to the subject as it is not meant to show a parade of learning[3] or to cause wonder : "Good Heavens! Did he read all that?"[4]

There should be a list of unprinted sources, which gives a clear account of the collections which have been used, where they are to be found, and what, if any critical problems they raise. There should also be a bibliography, or list of printed books, giving in each case the data and place of publication of the actual edition consulted. A bibliography, may have a secondary object, that of recording in general the existence of relevant literature for the use of other scholars. The desire to do this may not impair the primary objective, especially one is not supposed to include in the bibliography the book which have not been read just to suggest that the work is based on wider knowledge.[5]

The bibliography is generally made out by picking up titles out of the footnotes given in the book or dissertation but there is a change in the arrangement and order in the bibliography. In the footnote the author's name is mentioned straight and page number of the book or article is given : Romila Thapar, *Asoka and the Decline of the Mauryas,* OUP Oxford, 1961/1997, p.95. The bibliography is drawn author-wise in alphabetical order. The author's surname appears first, then the first name; the title of the work and the place as well as year of publication and the edition is mentioned. And there is no need to give page number:

Thapar, Romila, *Asoka and the Decline of the Mauryas,* OUP. Oxford, 1961/ revised edn. OUP, Delhi, 1997.

Types of Bibliography

There are three types of bibliography used in the books :

1. It is a kind of general bibliography, where a single list is arranged alphabetically by authors' names. It indicates the books, articles, newspapers, etc. used and consulted for the work.
2. The second type of bibliography is given under the title 'Select Bibliography' which indicates that only valuable works have been included. They are arranged according to the materials used and may be called "Classified Bibliographies." The sub-divisions may be made according to the sources used viz., Primary sources and the Secondary sources or between manuscripts and printed materials or between books and periodicals.[6] Some books include the titles of articles after the names of books if they are by the same author while in other books a list of articles is preferred separately. However, some authors have preferred to give the bibliography, dividing it according to the subject-matter treated in the book.
3. A third type of bibliography is termed as "Annotated Bibliography" which is a rare kind as it involves a more laborious procedure and critical knowledge of the subject. The author gives his critical remarks about the each book which finds mention therein. It may take the form of an essay and may serve as a critique on the subject. It is usually convenient

to divide this kind of bibliography chapter-wise or subject-wise. In case it is divided chapter-wise; it may further be sub-divided by subjects, in the order in which they are covered in the text. A bibliographical essay may be made readable but must be informative and critical. Without a critical judgement it has little worth for the readers.[7]

The form of bibliography is virtually dictated by the subject in your hand. "The type of bibliography you select to draw up for your work is therefore not something you can decide about before you are well past the mid-point of your research."[8]

Notes

1. G. Kitson Clark, *Guide for Research Students Working on Historical Subjects,* pp. 33 – 34.
2. *Ibid.,* p. 35.
3. *Ibid.,* pp. 32 – 33.
4. Barzun and Graff, *The Modern Researcher,* p. 292.
5. G. Kitson Clark, *op. cit.,* p. 32.
6. Barzun and Graff., *op. cit.,* p. 292.
7. *Ibid.,* pp. 293 – 294.
8. *Ibid.,* p. 295.

Additional References

Andhra Pradesh History Congress- Souvenir, 22nd session, 10th - 11th January, 1998, Department of History, University of Hyderabad.

History Teaching in India : Perspectives and Programmes for the Eighties (1976), University Grants Commission, New Delhi, 1978.

Journal of the Royal Asiatic Society, CUP, Third series, Vol-8, Part 3, Nov. 1998.

Pre-Historic and Early Historic Settlement Patterns in Andhra Predesh upto A.D. 500, M. Lavanya, An unpublished Ph.D. Thesis, University of Hyderabad, 1998.

The Indian Express–Relevant Articles.

The Indian Historical Review, Volume-II, Numbers 1-2, Ghaziabad, 1978-79.

University of Hyderabad, Doctoral Theses : 1982 to 1997.

SELECT BIBLIOGRAPHY

Agarwal, R.S, *Important Guidelines on Research Methodology,* Delhi, 1983.

Allchin, F.R., *The Archaeology of Early Historic South Asia,* CUP, 1995.

Altekar, A.S., *The Gupta Gold Coins in the Bayana Hoard,* Bombay, 1954.

Ashtana, Shashi, *Pre-Harappan Culture of India and The Borderlands,* New Delhi, 1985.

Barzun, Tacques, Graff, Henry F. *The Modern Researcher,* Third Edition, New York, 1977

Basham, A.L., *The Wonder that was India,* Indian edition, Bombay, 1963.

Basham, A.L. (ed.). *A Cultural History of India,* OUP Delhi, First Edn, 1975, Tenth Impression 1996.

Bhandarkar, D.R. *Lectures on Ancient Indian, Numismatics,* 1921, Reprinted Patna, 1984.

Brown, Richard & Daniels, Christopher W., *Learning of History,* London, 1986

Butterfield, Herbert *The Whig Interpretation of History,* New York, 1965

Carr, E.H., *What is History?* Penguin, England, 1965

Chattopadhyaya, Debiprasad (ed.) *History and Society*, Calcutta, 1978.

Chopra, P.N. (ed.) *The Gazetteer of India,* Vol II, History and Culture, Publications Division, Govt. of India, New Delhi, 1973.

Clark, G. Kitson, *Guide for Research Students Working on Historical Subjects* CUP, Cambridge, 1972.

Collingwood, R.G., *The Idea of History,* OUP London, First Edition, 1946, Reprinted 1973.

Cross, Rupert and Jones, P. Asterley, *An Introduction to Criminal Law,* London, second edition 1949

Denzin, Norman K.; *Images of Post Modern Society*, London, First Edition 1991, Reprinted 1993.

Devahuti (ed.) *Problems of Indian Historiography,* Delhi, 1979.

Dutta, Mala, *A Study of the Satavahanas Coinage,* New Delhi, 1990.

Elton, G.R., *The Practice of History,* London, 1967.

Fowler, H.W and Fowler, F, *The Concise Oxford Dictionary,* O U P London, First Edition 1911, Reprinted 1959.

Gardiner, Patrick, *The Philosophy of History,* OUP London, First Edition 1974 Reprinted 1984.

Ghosh, B.N., *Lectures on Scientific Method,* New Delhi, 1986

Gibaldi, Joseph and Schtert, Walter S., MLA Handbook for Writers of Research Papers, New Delhi, Third edition 1989.

Gopal, S. and Thapar, R. (eds.) *Problems of Historical Writing in India,* Proceedings of the seminar held at the India International Centre, New Delhi, 21st -25th January 1963.

Gottschalk, Louis, *Understanding History,* New York, Second Edition, 1969.

Gupta, P., *Geography from Ancient Indian Coins and Seals,* New Delhi, 1989.

Gupta, P.L., *Coins,* New Delhi, 1969.

Habib, Irfan, *Interpreting Indian History,* North-Eastern Hill University, Shillong.

—, *Essays in Indian History : Towards A Marxist Perception,* New Delhi, 1995.

Harvey, David, *The Condition of Post Modernity,* Cambridge, First Edition 1990, Reprinted 1994.

Hook, Sidney (ed.), *Essays in Social History and Philosophy and History* (A symposium) Oxford 1974.

Iggers, George G., *New Directions in European Historiography,* 1st Edition, 1975, Revised Edition, 1984.

Jacobson, Jerome (ed.), *Studies in the Archaeology of India and Pakistan,* New Delhi, 1986.

Jenkins, Keith, *Rethinking History,* London, 1991

Kalyanaraman, S., *Saraswati (Sindhu) Civilization, Saraswati,* Sindhu Research Centre, Chennai,1997.

Kosambi, D.D., *Indian Numismatics,* New Delhi, 1981.

Macdonell, Arthur A., *A History of Sanskrit Literature,* Delhi, Second Indian Edition 1971, Reprinted 1986.

Majumdar, R.C., *Historiography in Modern India,* Bombay, 1970.

Majumdar R.C. and Altekar A.S. (eds.), *The Vakataka - Gupta Age* Circa 200-550 A.D, Delhi, First Edition 1967, Reprinted 1986.

Marwick, Arthur., *The Nature of History,* London, First Edition 1970, Reprinted 1976.

Mc Cullagh, C. Behan, *The Truth of History,* London, 1998.

Mehta, R.N., *Medieval Archaeology,* Delhi, 1979.

Misra, R.P., *Research Methodology: A Handbook,* New Delhi, 1989.

Nevins, Allan, *The Gateway to History,* Bombay, Indian Reprint 1968.

Nugent, Walter T.K, *Creative History,* New York, 1967.

Pandey, Janak (ed.), *Social Reality,* Perspectives and understanding, New Delhi, 1988.

Popper, Karl. P., *Objective Knowledge: An Evolutionary Approach,* OUP, Revised Edition, 1986.

Rajannan, Busnagi. *Fundamentals of Research,* ASRC, Hyderabad, 1968.

Ranchhoddas, Ratanlal and Thakore, Dhirajlal Keshavlal, *The Law of Evidence* Bombay, Second Edition 1923.

Ray, Reba, *Ancient Settlement Patterns in Eastern India,* Calcutta, 1987.

Read, Carveth, *Logic-Deductive and Inductive,* London, Second Edition 1901.

Samerel, Raphael (ed.), *People's History and Socialist Theory,* London, 1981.

Saraswati, Baidyanath, *Pottery-Making Cultures and Indian Civilization,* New Delhi, 1978.

Sarup, Lakshman., *The Nighantu and the Nirukta,* Delhi, Reprinted , 1984.

Sastri, Nilakanta K.A., *A History of South India,* OUP , Third Edition, 1966, Second Impression 1971.

Sharan, M.K., *Tribal Coins–A Study,* Delhi, 1972.

Sharma, R.S., *Survey of Research in Economic and Social History of India,* ICSSR, Delhi, 1986.

Sharma, T.R., *The Concept of History,* Delhi, 1987.

—, *A Political History of Imperial Guptas* , New Delhi, 1989.

Sharma, Vidyadhar and Shastri, Madan Mohan *et al.* (eds.) *Nitya-Karma-Prayoga,* Gita Press, Gorakhpur, First Edition 1943, Nineteenth Edition 1988.

Sinha, B.P., *Archaeology and Art of India,* Delhi, 1979.

Sinha, B.P.,(ed.), *Potteries of Ancient India,* Patna, 1970.

Sircar, D.C., *Studies in Indian Coins,* Delhi, 1968.

Stern, Fritz (ed.), *The Varieties of History: From Voltaire to the Present,* London, First Edition, 1956.

Thapar, Romila, *A History of India I,* Penguin, England, First Edition, 1966, Reprinted, 1982.

—, *The Past and Prejudice,* New Delhi, 1973.

—, *Asoka and the Decline of the Mauryas,* OUP, Delhi, First 1961, Revised Edition, 1997.

—, *Ancient Indian Social History,* New Delhi 1978, Reprinted, 1987.
—, *Interpreting Early India,* OUP, Delhi First Edition 1992, Fourth Impression, 1997.
—, *Time as a Metaphor of History: Early India,* OUP, Delhi, First Edition, 1996. Second Impression, 1997.
Weber, Max., *The Methodology of the Social Sciences,* New York, 1949.
Webster, John C.B., *An Introduction to History:* Delhi, 1977.
Wojtasiewicz, Olgierd, *Methodology of History,* USA, 1973.

INDEX